COUNTRY LIFE BOOK OF
QUEEN ELIZABETH
The Queen Mother

Godfrey Talbot

Foreword by
HRH The Prince of Wales
KG, KT, PC, GCB

COUNTRY LIFE BOOKS

Author's acknowledgments

Much of my professional life has been spent in speaking and writing about the British Royal Family, playing the commentating broadcaster's part of 'instant historian'. Many thousands of miles of travel with royal parties all over the world, inside views and front seats on important occasions – good fortune has given me these, and thus accumulations of first-hand knowledge.

But a licensed communicator is not necessarily a professional biographer. Weaving the scripts of such a book as this is an undertaking which has brought new duties and demands, especially the responsibilities which come with the permanence of the printed word, essentially different from the ephemeral nature of the spoken word broadcast on the air waves. A writer must take time, dig deep, consult and check. Which is what I have tried to do.

The book and I are beholden to many people, firstly to the Prince of Wales. It is an honour again to have the Foreword written by His Royal Highness.

Above all, I would like to express enduring thanks to Queen Elizabeth The Queen Mother herself for once more giving her gracious permission – and her time to me and to the cameras – for facts and photographs. New pictures have been taken specially. They appear on the jacket and as frontispiece of this completely new edition of a book which has enjoyed Her Majesty's co-operation ever since its first emergence over ten years ago. This edition is the third major version of the book: it has acquired grandchild status.

Not that the continuing interest which The Queen Mother and her Household have given to this life story means that it is an 'official' biography, or that it has been dictated or censored. I have consulted many people in pursuit of accuracy, but the text's interpretations and opinions are mine.

Sincere gratitude goes to Sir Martin Gilliat, Sir Alastair Aird, Major John Griffin, Sir Ralph Anstruther, Mr. Robin Janvrin, and Lord Napier and Ettrick; also to the offices of the Prince of Wales, the Lord Chamberlain, the archives at Windsor Castle and the royal estates at Sandringham and in Scotland. Particularly, to my friend Robert Owen, veteran publisher and editor and writer – a father figure of the book.

GODFREY TALBOT

This edition first published in 1989 by
Country Life Books, an imprint of
The Hamlyn Publishing Group Limited,
a division of The Octopus Publishing Group,
Michelin House, 81 Fulham Road
London SW3 6RB

Copyright © Godfrey Talbot 1989

ISBN 0 600 55704 9

Produced by Mandarin Offset
Printed in Shekou, China

CONTENTS

KENSINGTON PALACE

Perhaps one of the most difficult things anyone can be asked to do is to write the foreword to a book about their grandmother. I can only admit from the very start that I am hopelessly biased and completely partisan, so that anyone expecting a "balanced" introduction to this book should either put it down at once or turn the page with suitable rapidity.

On the other hand, however many pages they turn over they will probably very quickly discover that the author of this book is equally and unashamedly partisan in his approach to his subject! But I don't think it will make any difference at all, for I suspect that the vast majority of people who acquire this book will have equally partisan views and will therefore have already fallen under the spell of the sparkling fascinating lady to whom this book is devoted.

I would have said that most grandsons probably have a rather special relationship with their grandmothers, which is no doubt something to do with the difference in generations, but ever since I can remember, my grandmother has been the most wonderful example of fun, laughter, warmth, infinite security and, above all else, exquisite taste in so many things. For me, she has always been one of those extraordinarily rare people whose touch can turn everything to gold - whether it be putting people at their ease, turning something dull into something amusing, bringing happiness and comfort to people by her presence or making any house she lives in a unique haven of cosiness and character. She belongs to that priceless brand of human beings whose greatest gift is to enhance life for others through her own effervescent enthusiasm for life. She has been doing that for almost nine decades, through war and peace, through change and uncertainty - an inspiration and a figure of love and affection for young and old alike.

You only have to look at the pictures in this book to see what an impact she has made on her century.

CHAPTER ONE

STAR OF THE CENTURY

'It wasn't what *I* did: it was us, together.'

HER MAJESTY once said that when speaking of her Queen Consort years. It was during a conversation when the present writer was researching for the first edition of this book, trying to get the facts right from the right person, the 'Queen Mum' – to use the affectionate accolade which the world has long given to Queen Elizabeth The Queen Mother.

That 'Us, together' remark of hers meant 'The King and I'. It was a characteristic playing down of her own importance, on being asked questions about her support for a hesitant husband during the fifteen years when the reluctant but courageous King, George the Sixth, having been thrust upon the Throne by a brother's abdication in 1936, was enabled to become a wise constitutional Sovereign with the help of a wonderful wife.

But with that phrase, 'Us, together', Her Majesty might well have been speaking not only of a marital partnership but of herself and her times, her match with the twentieth century whose years and her own number precisely the same. Their decades have marched together.

The Queen Mother's story is a golden thread in the tapestry of this century, her leadership a shining history in itself. She has, warrantably, adored her role. And it is hard for a chronicler, however clinical a reporter he may try to be, not to give the impression of adoring *her* and seem like some misty-eyed scrivener in a Clarence House Camelot. It is however not smoke, but smile that gets in your eyes. For this radiant Queen is a fascinating human being as well as a fine example. The quintessence of monarchy, yes, but the passions and frailties of us all are there in this royal symbol. Above all, though, is the courage and the dependability, with standards upheld and sadness never worn upon the sleeve. The finest Queen Consort in British history.

In her, monarchy is neither an anachronism nor a yawn. Child of the Victorian age, her light shines through nine decades; and she has made 'octogenerian' just a word.

Opposite One of the eighty-seventh birthday studies taken by Lord Snowdon at Clarence House, adjoining St. James's Palace, London home of Queen Elizabeth The Queen Mother.

All through the century she has been deep in good causes, has encouraged the better kind of social revolutions which have taken place, whilst savouring the nicenesses of life and turning an influential back on the awfulnesses. To her, it is as though life has been a large and lovely garden to move through, however pernicious the patches of weed may be. And what an extraordinary span of years – just by measurement but also by the undreamed-of things that have happened. She began her existence in pony-and-trap days, but she has lived into an age of arrow-speed flying and the penetration of outer space. As the years went on she herself became, and has remained, a zestful and pioneer patron of every transport development. When they arrived, helicopters were her natural conveyances and she has regularly been seen hopping in and out of them with the greatest enjoyment. She was the first royal person to take jet-propelled aircraft round the world. And when she became 85 years old she was given a special air-traveller's salute: she was wafted aboard a British Airways Concorde and treated to a gourmet luncheon high in the skies, and then sat in the pilot's cockpit to break the sound barrier. The two-hour flip round the United Kingdom and far out over the Atlantic was her most relished birthday present of that year.

So the background of her royal decades has changed immensely, its alterations far more drastic than most lifetimes encompass. Despite the past advances in travel and technology, many of the changes can hardly be seen to be for the better. An Empire has vanished; Britain is a great power in the world no more; thrones have toppled – though no passing of Hapsburg dynasties has worried *her*. Much more saddening must be the passing of many human decencies and many of the responsibilities of family life in the society of her homeland. Hardly anywhere is the picture like the scene when she was young. Violence has stamped inner cities which are multi-racial Babylons; vast stretches of countryside have become unlovely beneath the farm-field incursions of machinery and urban spillovers; old cottages sprout the metal sticks of television aerials; sudden skyscrapers block the sunlight even near Buckingham Palace, neighbour now to the pizza parlours and monster muzak halls of a micro-chip world. Loveless, lustreless.

But the Queen Mother's light glows on, untarnished, amid the surrounding vulgarities of life as the century nears an end. To

Opposite From the Saloon at Royal Lodge, five French windows like this one lead to the broad terrace and magnificent views of the house's lawns and woodlands.

Below The spacious and comfortably furnished Octagon Room at Royal Lodge has the Queen Mother's desk in the corner, where she can see the path beside her loved rose garden.

take a glance through the long list of her patronages is to know that, quite personally and practically, there is no despair in her, no inaction or indifference to the difficulties the century has brought. One thing that has not changed is her character; and to many people she has long been – often in a purely emotional way – a 'good influence' and a reassurance through times of national trouble and turbulence. Millions of families are possessive about her, not merely because of the longevity of a favourite Grannie but because the very image of her – the royal lady of the smile, the good sense and good manners and cheerful clothes – is an Eddystone beaming clear above the murky tides of politics. A kindly light. Something to keep.

This book is a celebration of Her Majesty, a completely new edition of a publication which has been in popular circulation for over ten years. Many of the original illustrations and chapters of the narrative are here again. Retained also, incidentally, is the style by which references to the Queen Mother in the text are as 'Queen Elizabeth', for that is how she is known to her family and her personal Household, whereas her reigning daughter is called quite simply 'The Queen'.

The Prince of Wales's Foreword once more graces the book. His words are a grandson's gleaming tribute to a fascinating lady. . . . Of whom there is much new to tell.

Her Majesty Queen Elizabeth the Queen Mother is of course by many years the senior representative of the dynastic House of Windsor; she is matriarch of what is now a large and still burgeoning clan, four generations of them. Naturally, then, the following pages cover, chronologically, the Queen Mother story from the growing-up of Elizabeth of Glamis to the growing-up of her great-grandchildren, the third one of whom, the already self-

Above Favourite pets, the famous corgis, crowd round the Queen Mother for chocolate snacks. The Queen is a spectator.

Opposite, top This was a church visit, down London's river, to St. Mary le Bow, but the visitor shared a moment with pearly Queens.

Opposite, bottom 'Look, she has come out!' Birthday well wishers at the gates of Clarence House.

assured boy prince, William of Wales, is second in line to the Throne.

The story is a panorama of a whole family and a whole nation. Great events of the century's history are a natural part of it, and the Queen Mother's own kin prominent in the pictures: the reigning Queen, second Elizabeth, and her children and their children; and the Gloucesters and the Kents; and now the new Yorks – all the immediate relatives, with a special glow surrounding those incomers-by-marriage, Diana and Sarah, whose weddings in the Eighties have been fairy stories for a listening and watching world. There are glimpses, too, of other and sometimes much more solemn state occasions; and of the experienced professionals who organize them, the essential officers of the royal Households who master the machinery of the Monarchy but who back discreetly from the ever more fierce light which beats upon the Throne in a Television Age whose mass-media coverage of 'the Royals' is a stupefying growth industry.

The palaces and the castles, they appear also: the royal homes with their gardens and farms, the stables and kennels: you

cannot easily get the British First Family into focus without their horses and dogs. Nor, for that matter, can you have the right view without a notion of the *work* the members of this family do. Top people they may be, but they are in no way idlers riding upon a nation's back.

A family saga, then. The tone of it set by this unique Queen Elizabeth, the lady of the tiaras and the feathered hats and the brightly-coloured clothes which match the smile, who has so often been seen as a shimmering star in ceremonial London but who is exactly the same human being who has been, through the years, observed off-duty at Sandringham or in Scotland, a fresh-air enthusiast happily marching out in the rain, wearing a comfortable old mac and pulled-on felt hat. The very stuff of plumed royalty and, equally, the genuine down-to-earth countrywoman.

She has played her star part in four reigns – as the enlivening daughter-in-law of George V, the sister-in-law of the man who was Edward VIII for eleven months, the undaunted Consort of George VI, and the matchless mother of Elizabeth II.

The Queen Mother has passed on to her daughter her own clear grasp of a Sovereign's place in the modern state, and the self-dedication needed for the inherited task. Above all, she has steered a good course, made monarchy human and the House of Windsor liked. In the post-Abdication ebb of the late Thirties, she probably *saved* the Throne.

And personally a tonic – she has always been that: infectiously lively and interested, fun to be with and to photograph (though averse to frolics for the sake of television programmes). Without putting on acts or strutting on footlit stages, she has nevertheless long been, by patronage and manifest enjoyment of performances, a prime star of the worlds of the theatre, ballet, middlebrow music, and 'command' variety. Her mark lies also upon the halls of universities and the Inns of Court. Versatility indeed.

The most popular owner in National Hunt racing too. Who else would have the bookies' 'blower' telephone bringing hot news from the courses into her own sitting room? Who but she never fails to include even the lowest stable lad on her Christmas-present list?

A whole fund of stories suggests that the art of the unpredictable comes naturally to her. What relief and enchantment it was, for instance, to nervous dinner-guests arriving very late at her door – after a car breakdown – to be told by their hostess: 'Don't apologise. I've been able to watch the whole of "Dad's Army" on the Box.' And what joy for an office staff's also-rans, squashed at the back of the entrance hall when Her Majesty came to open their new building, to see the visitor swing away from the oily tycoons lining the ordained red carpet and march into the crowd to say hello to typists and backstairs porters.

Wherever she is, she seems to be there *naturally*, part of a pleasant side of life. Most people alive today cannot remember a time when she was *not* visibly glowing in the pattern of public events. She has been Queen Mother for over half a lifetime. Yet before that, as a royal duchess and the Consort, as older citizens can recall, there were also the long spans of service through years of war and peace in whose ferment she was an influential figure, caring and durable, shaping the style and appeal of the Royal Family both then and as we know it today. Indeed, those perhaps were her 'finest hours'.

But the story begins at her own and the century's start.

LADY ELIZABETH LYON   HON^{BLE} DAVID LYON   HON^{BLE} ALEXANDER LYON

LADY MARY LYON

DOROTHY LADY GLAMIS   LADY ROSE LYON   CLAUDE, 14TH EARL OF STRATHMORE   CECILIA, COUNTESS OF STRATHMORE

PATRICK LORD GLAMIS   HON^{BLE} MICHAEL LYON

Remembrance of Queen Elizabeth's early days in Scotland comes from this portrayal of a family gathering at Glamis Castle. She, a young Elizabeth Bowes-Lyon then, is in the foreground with favourite brother David. Her parents, the Earl and Countess of Strathmore, take tea at the nearby table.

CHAPTER TWO

A COUNTRY CHILDHOOD

THE EVENTS and impressions of the very outset of Her Majesty's life are a story in themselves. First, it is odd that, bearing descent as she does from great and well-documented forebears, a small uncertainty remains in the record of the first hours of her own life. Not a mystery over parentage or the birth *date*: that was August 4, 1900. The imprecision arises over just *where* Elizabeth Angela Marguerite Bowes-Lyon first drew breath. We really don't know. Historians may ferret around the point, but 'it is of no matter' – the lady herself leaves it at that, a misleading birth-certificate notwithstanding.

Indeed the child was not 'news', not publicly important at the time. There was certainly no expectation that this baby would become a world figure. She was the ninth offspring, youngest but one, of the eldest son of a landowning peer not widely known. By ancestry and ambience a true and noble Scot.

But by birth – it is now admitted – a Londoner, born *somewhere* in the capital (one idea aired is that she was born in a hospital). In London anyhow. Her parents, Lord and Lady Glamis – who became the fourteenth Earl and Countess of Strathmore when Elizabeth was three – had an Adam house in St. James's and the family had relatives nearby. So probably the baby first saw the light of day through a house window in the heart of the city. But she was quickly removed to the country.

Until recent years it had always been thought, with reason, that the birthplace was actually the Strathmores', the Bowes-Lyons', rural mansion in Hertfordshire, St. Paul's Walden Bury. That was where her cradle was installed in the first days of her existence. The house was a big rambling Georgian house of warm redbrick, not many miles from what is now the busy new town of Stevenage. That is where Lady Elizabeth was brought up – though in the same breath it also has to be said that a good deal of her childhood and youth was spent far to the northward: in Scotland. Much of her training and her character came from historic Glamis Castle, the family's famous home which lies in a green valley situated between the Firth of Tay and the foothills of the Grampians.

There was Streatlam Castle in county Durham too, the great

house (demolished now) which had belonged to the Bowes side of the family. Happy girlhood days were spent there too; and Her Majesty retains to this day an affectionate association with Durham. Up at Streatlam and up at Glamis Elizabeth enjoyed long summers and autumns in the very early years of the century.

Not that St. Paul's Walden, the southern house, was anything but an enjoyed and always cherished home. It possessed – and still does – a tranquil rural air, with grounds extensive enough to make it seem far removed from towns. It dispensed a delightful pastoral charm, and the house itself had an enticing jumble of old outbuildings and garden nooks which made it a magical place for children to play and grow up in – even if it was not as exciting in a dramatic way as the other home, Glamis.

Lady Elizabeth's father, though he spent much of his time dutifully up there in Scotland, must himself have been obsessively attached to the Hertfordshire house – with little thought for London – because in 1900 when, as the male parent, he officially logged the arrival of this new daughter, the entry which he made in the Registrar's office in Hitchin declared that the birth*place* was 'St. Paul's Walden Bury'. Not quite true also is the engraved plaque in the chancel of the local All Saints church, perpetuating the small falsehood. The words carved in the tablet are correct, however, in stating that the baby was *baptized* in that church.

The Lord Glamis of that summer in the year 1900 does seem to have been forgetful, and then in a hurry, over the infant's documentation, for he was extraordinarily late about the business: six whole weeks, indeed, after the regulation period allowed for the registration of a birth. When at last the notification reached the proper office it was only two days before the day of the child's christening.

That formal recording of a birth might have been more prompt and precise if Elizabeth's mother rather than her father had seen to the paper work. She was a very practical as well as a very pleasant person, probably the most sweetly redoubtable Lady Strathmore in the whole Bowes-Lyon family history, shrewd and serene at the same time, artistic, musically talented, a good needlewoman and a brilliant gardener. Formerly Miss Nina Cecilia Cavendish-Bentinck, kinswoman of the dukes of Portland, she had inherited a flair for endearing herself to young

Opposite *The youngest Bowes-Lyon children, Elizabeth and David, loved 'dressing up'.*

Top *Elizabeth and David build a house of cards in the Bowes-Lyons' Hertfordshire house, St. Paul's Walden Bury.*

Bottom *From the family album: Lady Elizabeth on 'Bobs', her cherished pony.*

Left *The Garden Room at St. Paul's Walden Bury, more usually known as the Red Room, is today much as it was during the early years of Lady Elizabeth Bowes-Lyon.*

people and encouraging her children in the gentlest way to enjoy duties, and service to others, as a natural part of existence. 'Life is for living,' she would say. 'Work is the rent you pay for life; and if you're bored, the fault is in yourself.'

There was nothing boring about St. Paul's Walden, where the small Elizabeth spent so much of her time in the sunlit Edwardian years. Life was warm and busy and free in the old house where magnolias and honeysuckles climbed the walls deliciously and the woods and shrubberies were full of enchantments.

Her constant companion was the youngest of the family, her much loved brother David Bowes-Lyon, born two years after she was. They were always together: their mother called them 'my two Benjamins' and she enjoyed the reference to the name of the youngest of Jacob's twelve sons in the Bible story. The pair were so much younger than all the other brothers and sisters that Lady Strathmore used to say that people sometimes mistook them for her grandchildren.

Elizabeth and David played games and kept pets – indoors as well as outdoors, not only in the main house itself. One favourite haunt was 'the Flea House', an ancient and long disused brew house in which they secretly laid in rations and held hidden picnics. When they were corralled for lessons their schoolroom was the nursery, the place where they scribbled their first arithmetic on scratchy slates and read their first books curled up in front of the fireplace's high brass fender. They had pets galore: puppies, kittens, chickens, ring-doves. Animals seemed to be all over the place; and one particularly favourite companion and

mount was a Shetland pony called Bobs who used to follow the small girl indoors as well as out, even up and down staircases.

Special tenderness was lavished on small birds, and the children even tamed bullfinches. Whenever a dead bird was discovered, in explorations of the lawns and woodlands of the estate, it received a solemn burial in a little box lined with rose leaves. No wonder the Queen Mother has been essentially a countrywoman all her life, thoroughly at home in meadows and on moors, responding always to the joys of flower-filled country gardens such as those in which St. Paul's Walden was embowered. Down at the Hertfordshire house – indeed wherever those two young hedonists were living – the fresh-air influence of the unpretentious, romping family to which they belonged was strong.

But in those early years nobody had a greater impress on their characters than a 'most wonderful woman' (David Bowes-Lyon's description) called Clara Knight, Elizabeth's formidable nurse. Mrs. Knight (the 'Mrs.' was the customary courtesy title, even though Clara was for all her life a spinster) was the daughter of a tenant farmer on one of the Strathmore estates. She was always known as 'Allah' because that was the nearest the children could get to pronouncing the name Clara. One of the finest of the old type of sturdy nanny, she was quiet, high principled, tenderly strict, very professional and very loyal, completely in control of her young charges and their paddywhacks, dependable day and night whether parents were at home or away, an unruffled goddess of nursery parties and perambulator parades. She served generations of Strathmores,

Above *During the early years of this century the children of the fourteenth Earl and Countess of Strathmore frequently played in and around the barns and pre-sixteenth-century granary (centre).*

Left *At the back of St. Paul's Walden Bury; looking down on the barns and granary is the old clock tower, and belfry.*

Opposite *King George V – as he later was – with some of his young family on the Sandringham estate early in the century.*

going off to mother the little Elphinstones when Elizabeth's eldest sister married Lord Elphinstone and had young of her own. In her turn, Elizabeth, when much later she was Duchess of York, stole the old treasure to look after her own first baby.

Back in Elizabeth's young girlhood days, education at home in the nursery classrooms proceeded agreeably under Lady Strathmore's personal supervision and Allah's loving eye. At no stage of early childhood or adolescence did she go away to school (except for a couple of short terms during the beginning of teenage when attendances were made at a day establishment for young ladies in South Audley Street, London). Absorption of English, French, history, music and dancing went steadily forward under the tuition of a succession of governesses and specialist teachers, who found their pupil apt, lively – and mischievous. Tantrums and squabbles with 'elders and betters' were not unknown. But when 'best behaviour' was ordered it was beautifully done.

Callers at St. Paul's Walden in those days – horse-drawn or decanted from noisy new motor-cars – remembered how they sometimes found a smiling and self-possessed little person already peeping round the front door, ready to dance along the corridor and lead the way to the drawing-room where Lady Strathmore had rung for tea. Then Elizabeth, who had been summoned from the garden and 'made presentable' shortly before, would stand politely beside the teapot and engage in conversational pleasantries far beyond her years. The impressed visitors would have found it hard to believe that this was the same child who, with her brother, delighted in raiding the kitchen and smuggling not only cakes and buns, but matches and Woodbine cigarettes, into the grimy attic of the 'Flea House' where, remote from parents and staff and elder brothers and sisters, they would play at 'camping out' and 'withstanding

sieges'. In that loft, and other eyries, they would try to hide for hours, but usually laughed so much – or perhaps forgot that Woodbine smoke smelled – that they gave the hide-and-seek game away to adult searchers.

Life at St. Paul's Walden certainly left its stamp. But strongest of all influences on the daughter's nature and its joyfulness was the maternal one. There is no doubt that Lady Elizabeth (the style of 'Lady' was acquired when her father succeeded to the Strathmore earldom in 1904) learned more, and had her enduring character moulded more, by the daily personal contacts with her mother than by any of the professional educators who attended the schoolrooms.

Her devout father, a quiet and kindly country gentleman with a deep knowledge of rural affairs and concern for the welfare of his lands, was the unobtrusive parent. It was the Countess who presided notably and sympathetically over the large family; and she clearly had a *tendresse* for the youngest daughter (born when her elder sister Mary was seventeen). Lady Strathmore was an adored energizer. She sparked enthusiasm infectiously and deployed a host of skills and charms. She had a rare ear for music, would go to a concert and come back to her own piano and play the pieces perfectly. And she was also a fascinating raconteur, telling stories with gusto and gaiety, and with a great play of her hands. She made friends easily, had a complete lack of snobbery, but intuitive likes and dislikes. As were many mothers of the large families which were fashionable in Victorian times, she was a rarely-absent, wholesome presence to all her brood, though stricter – so the boys said – with the older children than with the young ones. And it is easy to believe the special affection shown to that Strathmore 'Benjamin', the quicksilver Elizabeth, the blue-eyed imp who came to resemble her mother in her wills and her ways all through her life.

Above *In the grounds of St. Paul's is this graceful and peaceful temple. The architect was Sir William Chambers (1726–96). The temple, which had stood in Dansen Park, Bexley Heath, was brought to St. Paul's by Sir David and Lady Bowes-Lyon in 1961.*

Right *All Saints church, St. Paul's Walden, where Lady Elizabeth was baptized.*

Opposite *Fine trees and old statuary on the sweep of lawn – a view of St. Paul's Walden Bury, some thirty miles north of London.*

CHAPTER THREE

ELIZABETH OF GLAMIS

ENGLISH-BORN, yes, and with an English mother, but it is beyond dispute that this girl who was to become a crowned Consort and a Queen Mother unique in history is a Scotswoman. By long heredity on her father's side, by upbringing during formative years in one of the great castle strongholds of the North, and by many facets of her character, the Scots are her ain folk.

True, there are other national and family strains to be traced. Even one line of descent from the last hero of the independent princes of Wales, Owain Glendwr. Also, through some forebears named Smith who emigrated in earlier centuries, a touch of North American ancestry, with the names of Robert E. Lee and George Washington written on that branch of the family tree.

But those are sidelines. By tradition and romance and reality, Her Majesty's Scottish stock sweeps other genealogy into the shade. Though not born royal, she possesses, through no less an ancestor than King Robert the Bruce, royal blood from the Northern Realm in her veins, and a pedigree not only as distinguished, but also as stirring, as anything in the history of the *English* Throne.

The house, great Glamis itself, looks like a fairy-tale castle with its towering turrets and battlements, but the impressive pile is more than real enough, a massive mansion of thick stone walls, decorative yet built for defence. One would have imagined that such a fortress belonged to the top of one of the nearby hills instead of the soft green valley where in fact it lies, set in the level fields and woodlands of a lovely stretch of the old county of Angus, twelve miles north of Dundee and four miles south of Kirriemuir. A nice legend cherished by old folk in the village is that in some dim and distant past their primitive ancestors did attempt to build a fortress on a local summit, but when the workmen returned each morning to the foundations they had laid on the previous day they found their wood and stone tumbled and widespread by the wee elfin people whose fairy-rings had been violated. For a while, the castle-builders reassembled their structures each day, only to have the night-time disarray repeated. At length they gave up, left the hilltops to the 'guid folk', and sited the stronghold in the flat Great Glen,

Opposite Lady Elizabeth photographed at the time of her betrothal to the Duke of York in January 1923.

the lowland spot where Glamis Castle stands today, solid and ancient.

Built into the warm pink stone are fragments of what was a royal hunting lodge in medieval times. The Queen Mother's long-ago predecessors received the ownership of the castle during the fourteenth century. It came to the family when Princess Joan, daughter of the Scots king, Robert II, married the tall and distinguished Sir John Lyon, Keeper of the Privy Seal, and called 'The White Lyon' because of his fair hair. Sir John became the Thane, the first Lord Glamis, acquiring lands which attended the title, but no great wealth. Money arrived in the family much later, well after the earldom of Strathmore and Kinghorne had been bestowed in Stuart times.

Not until the middle of the eighteenth century did that affluence enter the story. The nineteenth Lord Glamis (ninth Earl of Strathmore) married a certain Miss Mary Eleanor Bowes, only child and heiress of George Bowes, a very rich industrialist in County Durham. That is when the family name of Bowes-Lyon, as well as Mr. Bowes' fortune, came in. What happened is that the good George, who owned estates in Durham and in Hertfordshire too, made it a condition of the marriage endowment that the titled family should change their surname to Bowes. The Strathmores couldn't bear to abandon the old name altogether for long, however, and soon made it 'Lyon-Bowes', only half paying titular tribute to the dowry. And after the magnate's death, the present style of Bowes-Lyon was adopted.

It is said that the Queen Mother was never fond of the 'Bowes' name. People on the Glamis estate cherish stories of an uninhibited girl bouncing into cottage or village shop trilling, 'Hello, how are you? I'm Elizabeth Lyon'.

To think of the old Bowes side of the family as unlettered mine-owners and little more is to get the picture wrong, however. They were men of culture as well as coal. One of them, a John Bowes who was a son of the tenth Earl and flourished in the nineteenth century, left behind an extraordinary architectural monument and treasure house in the North of England. He and his French wife, an artist, collected paintings, furniture and ceramics in profusion, and this rich heritage can be seen today, assembled in all its magnificence within the Bowes museum near the town of Barnard Castle. The building itself, in the style of a

Above *Lord and Lady Strathmore with their children. Lady Elizabeth, a small girl, stands by her mother.*

Right *Through the centuries Glamis has been visited and lived in by many members of the Scottish and British Royal Families. Princess Margaret was born here. The illustration shows the Queen Mother's sitting room, preserved as in her young days.*

massive French château, is an astonishing sight to find at the edge of remote Durham moorlands, and is crammed with priceless exhibits from all over Europe, among them paintings by El Greco, Goya, Boucher, Courbet and Tiepolo. A lavish yet little-known legacy.

Queen Elizabeth, connoisseur of beautiful furnishings though she later became, would not have known much about the Museum in the early 1900s. She has been there in more recent times, and in 1982 officially opened three Second Empire galleries.

What the young girl did revel in, during the first dozen years of the present century, was the 'museum' which was her own home, the Castle itself, an ever-exciting dwelling to anyone who knew and relished history as she did. For here was history all around. Few inhabited castles can command echoes so romantic, so violent, so spine-chilling. Few so tenaciously housing legends of apparitions on regular parade: clanking warriors, chained-up monsters, fierce Earl Beardies round the corner and Grey Ladies in the chapel. Elizabeth lapped them all up, shivered with imagining, and played at 'being ghosts' with her brother. The reports from those days speak of pranks but not panic. Hers, it seems, was a spirit never cowed by the great mansion around her. Not even by theatrical claims linking Macbeth's murder of King Duncan with the strange patches on the stairs that were supposed to be inexpungeable bloodstains.

No, the great stone stairways and spooky attics were just perfect playgrounds for hide-and-seek, the armour and the axes and the shields on Glamis's stark walls only reminders of a turbulent past full of dark deeds which spiced childhood hours.

Not all the reminders were grim. Carefully preserved, for instance, was a watch of Bonnie Prince Charlie's: the Young Pretender left it ticking beside his bed at the castle when the English came after him by night and he had to flee in haste. But more exciting things than that inspired the children's pastimes, things like ancient battles and sieges. One favourite game – before David, to his sister's sorrow, went away to school – was 'repelling raiders' by pouring boiling oil down from a parapet upon new arrivals at the entrance to the castle. The 'oil' was buckets of cold water, but shock enough for unsuspecting visitors.

A story is told in Glamis village of one time when Elizabeth's sense of fun exploded in musical fashion. It was one afternoon when she had been having piano and organ instruction and went on to sit at the harmonium in the Castle chapel. (Her Majesty still remembers 'those awful pedals which you pumped to make the bellows work'.) The small fingers which had been plodding up and down the keys doing battle with a Handel voluntary suddenly played a chord full blast, changed the tempo and, to the accompaniment of squeaks of laughter from the young organist, the chapel resounded to a spirited version of 'Yip-i-addy-i-ay'!

A country child, a bundle of fun. But in the ballroom she was an ardently serious and certainly sophisticated young person,

Below *Of all the rooms at Glamis perhaps the Drawing Room, or Great Hall, is the most magnificent. Particularly interesting is the fireplace shown here, measuring thirteen-and-a-half feet in width and reaching to the spring of the ornate plasterwork ceiling, created in 1621. The vast canvas is of the third Earl with his sons.*

Left *A future home, though Elizabeth and her Prince 'Bertie' did not know it when they were young. White Lodge in Richmond Park became their first house as a married couple.*

Opposite *Glamis Castle.*

nicely drilled, toes like rhythmic thistledown. Even when only five years old her dance timing was a joy to be seen. Her bright social graces were proudly displayed at the age of eight when she was for the first time a bridesmaid, one of the chosen attendants at the wedding of her eldest brother to a duke's daughter in the Guards' Chapel at Wellington Barracks, London. Nor was she backward at telling everybody of the part she played in the ceremony!

Few children can have crowded so much in the first dozen years of life. Years of warm companionship, glorious fun and frolics. She worked hard enough in the schoolrooms and exams were successfully passed, but altogether life must have seemed sheer happiness, especially those months spent in Scotland in summertime when all the clan were together, the boys on holiday from school and university. There was cricket and tennis, energetic picnics and enthusiastic gardening. The family lived in the light and airy rooms of a wing built in the last century, well away from the old ghostly chambers with their echoing stone walls and floors. The windows looked out over the Dutch garden – and a new garden which everyone joined in creating under Lady Strathmore's direction and which was completed in 1910. These were green and golden years. The world's troubles and the worrying international situation under the clouds of German militarism did not intrude into the Bowes-Lyon country life. Not just then.

World War One

But swift and terrible change was coming – to Britain and to the Glamis people. And Elizabeth Bowes-Lyon will always remember how a darker chapter began in the second decade of her life. It began in fact during a visit to London on one of the special treats in town for important anniversaries. Usually these were occasions of delight, but this one proved to be a day of ominous drama.

August 4, 1914 it was. Her fourteenth birthday – and the date on which the Kaiser's War started. Although it was on the very night when the outbreak of hostilities was officially declared, Elizabeth's promised visit to a West End theatre was not cancelled. She sat with her family in a box at the Coliseum, and at the end of the variety performance, when the Britain-at-war news was solemnly announced from the stage, looked down on an audience which boiled with sudden patriotic excitement expressed in wild cheering. At midnight, home in bed in the Strathmores' London house, she could hear the roaring of the crowds going down the Mall and the streets around to gather in front of Buckingham Palace. They shouted for the King, George the Fifth, for four years their Sovereign and now leader of a nation embattled. It was a strident start to sombre days.

No staying in London, then. Quickly back went the birthday-party group, back to the quiet of Glamis. Elizabeth was to spend most of the First World War years in a castle – as, a quarter of a century later, her daughter, also a Queen-to-be, was to spend the World War Two years in another castle, royal Windsor. In 1914, chill and emptiness entered the life of the youngest Bowes-Lyons. Elizabeth's brothers, so very much older – the eldest was 30 and the youngest of those 'of age' was 21 – were quickly in soldier's uniform and away on active service. Not all were to return: Captain Fergus, in the Black Watch which was the family regiment, was killed in France at the battle of Loos in 1915, and Captain Michael, though he came through, was wounded, captured, and 'missing, reported dead' for most of the war.

Wounded men became part of Elizabeth's immediate life.

Opposite *Glamis Castle, owned by the Strathmores since 1372.*

Left *After the war, 'Bertie', Duke of York, visits Glamis. In this group, he stands behind the Lady Elizabeth he was courting. The Bowes-Lyon family surround them.*

Below *Lady Elizabeth and friends ready for a ride. (From the left) Lady Doris Gordon Lennox, Lord Settrington, Lady Elizabeth, the Hon. Bruce Ogilvy, the Earl of Haddington, Miss Alex Cavendish (seated) and the Hon. Diamond Hardinge.*

Queen Mary with the Duke and Duchess of York and Prince George, later the Duke of Kent, at Balmoral in September 1923.

Glamis Castle was turned into a convalescent hospital. Beds were lined up round the walls of the big dining room and the crypt saw new life as a dining hall. With the Countess tirelessly in charge, Elizabeth was her mother's right hand, tireless too. It was as though 1914 had turned the girl into a woman. She must have been the most hard-working, yet most cheerful, teenager in Scotland. Some schoolroom routine had to be kept up, but now there was sterner stuff to face when lessons were over. She was herself an assistant nurse.

With grim regularity, as the war ground on and casualties mounted, ambulances filled with maimed men in khaki or hospital blues came lumbering up from Dundee and over the Sidlaw Hills. And at Glamis many of the injured found healing and a lightening of heart too, so that when they had long left the castle they talked about their experiences there for the rest of their lives as Old Comrades scattered all over the British Isles and far away in Australia and New Zealand.

Whatever trepidation the wounded soldiers at first felt at being organized by a titled lady in a cold Scottish castle, the fear soon disappeared in the warm ambience of Lady Strathmore's personality and the twinkling charm of the young daughter. The radiant sympathy and tonic spirits of the girl with the fringe, and the infectious smile which seemed never to leave her, soon had the men competing for her company at the meal tables, soon had them begging for help in writing letters, playing cards, running sing-songs, sewing shirts, doing their bits of shopping. They would jostle for a place in her picnic-bound wagonette. She teased them, calling them all by Christian names, played the piano for 'Pack up Your Troubles' and 'Keep the Home Fires Burning'. They were guests in her mother's house, and Elizabeth, as junior hostess, was completely natural and at ease in her caring for them. One man said – as many in later generations have put it – 'You felt you were the one person in the world she wished to be with'.

Those servicemen who spent convalescence at Glamis were the first people outside her own circle to experience at close hand the entrancing character which the world was to know in years to come when that girl became a Queen.

In November 1918, four years after the beginning of the war, the Armistice was signed and fighting stopped. Not an end to sorrow, but blessed relief to a world sickened and bereft by the slaughter on the Somme. Presently there came the joy-and-sorrow departures of the last batches of soldiers from the Castle. And Elizabeth could spread her wings.

She was eighteen, assured and attractive. She had come to womanhood in anxious and unnatural times, though in the war's last year life had not been entirely devoted to nursing duties. There had been week-end visits to some of the great houses in Scotland and in the South for wedding celebrations and dances and the occasional full-dress parties which she loved. She had become an accomplished partner as well as hostess, never at a loss in quadrille or conversation. Most of her lessons had come easily to her: she already spoke French like a native. Friends noticed that a steady will of her own and self-control had come to match the ebullience of childhood.

So when this pretty girl went south once more and experienced, without plunging wildly into, the hectic Society of the early Twenties in London, she was much in demand. Life was busy and sweet in the first strawberries-and-cream-and-Ascot years, and greatly enjoyed. But popularity with the young men did not go to her head and she never sought to tie her beaux. She was not conceited: it was a natural thing to have a string of admirers. People have always been in love with her.

Yet the name of this Lady Elizabeth was still unknown to the public in England. Not even in small type was she in the Court and Social columns of the newspapers. It was her friendship – first of all through work as a Girl Guide commissioner – with Princess Mary, the daughter of King George and later known as the Princess Royal, which began her path to recognition and to royalty. She was invited to the Palace, met the King and Queen Mary, and also met the King's second son, Prince 'Bertie' – Albert, Duke of York. There had been a brief encounter between the two at a children's party when she was five and Bertie ten, but real acquaintance began only now, and gradually too.

The year 1920 saw the starting of the friendship. The Duke of York was emerging, though with a stiff shyness that was in contrast to Lady Elizabeth's relaxed spontaneity, from his own wartime rigours. The Royal Navy had been his career and, in spite of periods of ill health, he had served at sea as a junior officer and had been in action at the battle of Jutland in 1916 (leaping at once from sick-bay bunk to his gun-turret post for the whole major engagement). Persevering over physical frailties, he qualified as a pilot in the Flying Corps, tried his hand at a Civil Service desk, studied industrial welfare, and took a course in economics at Trinity College, Cambridge. He was a slim, good looking man, but far from being a self-confident extrovert full of small talk and humour such as many of Elizabeth's dance partners were. He envied people socially at ease and conversationally fluent. And he thought Elizabeth Lyon was wonderful.

Happily, because of a visit or two with his parents to the Strathmores, he had become a friend and shooting companion of the Bowes-Lyon brothers, and from time to time he went to stay at Glamis and at St. Paul's Walden Bury. He loved these visits. The family's free and easy life style, their unregimented jollity, the country house tennis, the after-dinner evenings of rollicking old songs round the piano – everything was marvellously different from life at his own home. The Court in which he had been brought up was positively Victorian. King George and Queen Mary were the most starchy of parents. The King's severe quarter-deck manner and fanatic insistence on punctuality and obedient behaviour made it virtually impossible for him to

It was a lovely wedding. This was the bride, Lady Elizabeth, leaving for the Abbey in the Spring of 1923.

The official wedding photograph of Their Royal Highnesses the Duke and Duchess of York, April 26, 1923.

communicate with his own children. As to them, their father's occasional attempts at forced jocularity made them even more frightened of him. And there was never such a thing as a young people's party at the Buckingham Palace of those days.

So the occasions when the Duke of York was able to escape and spend a while with the boisterous, welcoming Bowes-Lyons must have been almost intoxicatingly cheerful for that royal Second Son, bedevilled by nervousness and bouts of gloomy temper which stemmed from an intractable stammer – and an existence in the shadow of his glamorous elder brother, David, the Prince of Wales.

Life with the Lyons was a revelation and a joy. The sun was beginning to shine for that 'Bertie' in his middle twenties. No wonder his meetings with Lady Elizabeth were both stunning and stimulating. No wonder that even the hurried reports he gave to his father and mother suggested that he was 'coming out of his shell'. Elizabeth's effect on him began to dispel some of his hesitancy, and soon he was able to summon persuasiveness as he eagerly competed with her eternal circle of admirers for the pleasure of a dance. He was in love, and became for almost two years a suitor, even though he was often shyly in the background. Hopes of the possibility of a future with her rose when in 1922 she was one of the bridesmaids attending his sister Princess Mary at her marriage to Lord Lascelles, the future sixth Earl of Harewood.

To Queen Mary it was clear that Elizabeth would make an excellent wife for Bertie. Gruff King George with wisdom and truth declared: 'You'll be a lucky feller if she accepts you'.

The feller had to wait, and he was not altogether patien about it. But it was not the easiest thing in the world for the happy and sought-after girl to make her decision. The warmth and affection in her went out to Bertie. There was much in him that appealed: the integrity and innate courage, his modesty and devotion, the self-effacing manners and the high standards he set himself, and perhaps above all the way that resolution and even raillery entered his character when he was at her side. Yet she hesitated. To say yes would be to step out of her private world and the glow of an adorably informal family into not only the harsh limelight of public life and work, but also into a Court circle of routine much more cold and isolated than anything which characterizes British monarchy today. That side of the life which was being offered to her, the constraints of royalty – even though it was not Heir-to-the-Throne royalty – was uninviting.

But the Duke of York pressed his suit with steady persistence, and at last he was rewarded. She accepted. He won her heart. One Sunday morning early in 1923, as they walked in the St. Paul's Walden woodlands which had been the fairy playgrounds of Elizabeth's childhood, Prince Bertie, twenty-seven years old, proposed to the girl of his dreams, who was twenty-two then, and received the answer he had longed for. He dispatched, in code, a joyful telegram to the King and Queen at Sandringham; and three days later the Court Circular announced the betrothal.

The engagement came unheralded upon the public. Popular though Lady Elizabeth had become in the country houses and the society circles in which she had moved, she was not widely known. There were some headlines, to be sure, but the newspapers' scrambles for details about her were not very successful, and the betrothal reports were short. No posse of Fleet Street photographers descended upon St. Paul's Walden, for the manner of publicity was not feverish in those days. In any case, although here was the first of the Monarch's sons to become affianced, it was not this one but the eldest, his brother the Heir, who commanded journalistic attention. Press and public continued to concentrate on the debonair and dashing Prince of Wales, who had no inferiority complex, and one day would be King.

Even so, the reporters began to find out about the lady who was to wed the second Prince; their readers discovered that she was pretty and witty, intriguingly tender too. Well brought up, of course, nicely reserved and composed when that was needed, yet at the same time winningly impulsive and direct. Much more than just an upper-class deb.

As to the lady's family, it was typical of the Bowes-Lyons that their contentment was not so much that their Elizabeth was making a fine match as that she was marrying a good man for whom they had formed great liking.

The engagement was short and the wedding took place in Westminster Abbey on April 26, 1923. Two of the groom's brothers, the Prince of Wales and Prince Henry (the Duke of Gloucester) were his supporters. The bride, accepting one of the many still-strong Victorian traditions that such an occasion demanded a formidable retinue, had eight bridesmaids. Her dress was of deep ivory to match the colour of the venerable lace which Queen Mary had lent her. White roses of York and white heather of Scotland were in the bouquet she carried as she set off to church from the house in Bruton Street, Mayfair, to which her parents had moved.

Incidentally, few brides can have had their wedding day flowers in their hands for so short a time, for, once inside the Abbey's west door and waiting for the clergy to form-up in procession, she impulsively laid her bouquet on the floor's gravestone marking the tomb of the Unknown Warrior. One can readily imagine that, even at that moment on a happy day, memories of the war and the sight of that Warrior memorial which was then so new brought recollections of loss to Elizabeth's mind, and prompted the gesture. She walked to the altar without the bouquet – and began a tradition: at every royal wedding since, all through two following generations and over sixty years to the blazoned nuptials of grandsons Charles and Andrew, the bride's flowers have rested on that poppy-bordered Soldier's Stone. But have been placed there *after* the wedding day.

Remembered today, that Abbey marriage in 1923 is inevitably compared with all the later magnificent and magnified weddings; for instance, to those of her elder daughter, Elizabeth II, and her granddaughter Princess Anne twenty-four and fifty years afterwards, and of course the celebrations so bursting with pageantry which brought in the modern 'commoners' Diana Spencer and Sarah Ferguson much more recently. Royal weddings have become television spectaculars on a world scale, watched, at every moment of their happening, by scores of millions of people.

By such yardsticks, that entry of the Yorks into matrimony in the year 1923 was a low-key event in an old fashioned world. There was no broadcasting of it whatever. It happened long before television, and even B.B.C. radio was only one year old, though already full of endeavour. The Corporation did ask permission to put some of the wedding on the 'wireless' but the notion horrified the great church's authorities. Direct commentary and a relay of sound from inside the Abbey? No, such a thing had never been done, certainly not for a royal wedding. The Dean personally was no opponent of broadcasting, but his obscurantist Chapter refused intrusion by microphone, fearful that 'disrespectful people might hear the service, perhaps even some of them sitting in public houses with their hats on'!

The wedding was a popular event nevertheless. For one thing, it took minds off the prevalent industrial depression at home and the rumbling portents of international strife coming from Germany even then. In any case, this bride of good Scottish blood (an Anglo-continental monarchy was indeed ending) was bringing something very perceptibly new into the Royal Family: a smile. People quickly noticed and liked that; liked also the fact that, though State processions flowed from the church when the

A popular wedding picture taken on the day the Duke of York married Lady Elizabeth. The parents of the couple are with them.

Above *On their honeymoon the Duke and Duchess are seen leaving church after the morning service at Bookham, Surrey on April 29, 1923.*

Below *Golf at Polesden Lacey, where the first part of the honeymoon was spent.*

A studio portrait taken before Lady Elizabeth's marriage. Pearls remained part of the royal lady's picture, but the fringe was soon to disappear.

ceremony was over, Elizabeth had driven to the Abbey in an unpretentious landau with no such thing as a military escort. There were decorations and cheering crowds in the streets, though; and for London at least it was a day of festivity, and of history: this was the first wedding of a king's son at Westminster since a young Richard II married Princess Anne of Bohemia 540 years before.

So Elizabeth of Glamis became a Duchess and a Royal Highness. The King, who saluted her and Scotland by announcing that morning that the bridegroom was a Knight of the Thistle now, conferred the dignity of a Princess on her during the wedding breakfast, at which the newlywed needed all her strength and help from her husband to saw the first incision which began the attack upon a wedding cake nine feet high.

The honeymoon was spent at Polesden Lacey in Surrey, then the country home of Mrs. Ronald Greville, and at Glamis, where the weather was so bleakly uncivil that Her Royal Highness unromantically developed whooping cough. The Castle, for once, was not a tonic. Bertie, the gossips going up from the village said, suffered as much as 'our Princess' did – suffered from worry until the Elizabeth who was the loadstar of his life recovered.

CHAPTER FOUR

DUCHESS OF YORK

FROM HER first entry into royal life, the new Duchess found herself the object of much public inspection. She neither raised objections nor showed ostentation during the engagements which began to fill her diary. Carrying her new rank as though born to it, she took Press attention naturally and with modest surprise. She was courteous and helpful. Perhaps too kind. Once, in the very early days, when a reporter had called, she was what her father-in-law regarded as too informal and informative about herself and the Duke: the King went to the trouble of sending an equerry to ask that there should be no interviews in future.

George V had fixed ideas, rooted in a Victorian past, about almost everything, certainly on what ladies should do and indeed what they should wear. New styles, men's and women's, infuriated him. In his own clothing he stuck to the fashions of his youth, continuing to appear in hard hats, trousers creased at the sides, spats, and cloth-topped boots. It was said that he wore the same collar-stud, repeatedly repaired, for fifty years.

But his lively daughter-in-law patently captivated him. He quickened to her refreshing spirit in the same way as his wife, the normally undemonstrative Queen Mary, had done from the first. For her he relaxed the Palace's notoriously strict rules about punctuality, and, to the family's astonishment – for they'd always had to be at table and ready to start meals 'on the dot' – he merely smiled when one day Elizabeth arrived for dinner noticeably late and laughing her apologies. 'Not at all, my dear', he said. 'We must have sat down a few minutes too early.' She had a growing rapport with him, far warmer than anything which existed between the Monarch and his own offspring. The young Duchess seemed instinctively to understand his ingrained need of orderliness and his respect for routine and tradition. In this, she was the antithesis of her brother-in-law, the Prince of Wales, who was in an almost perpetual state of suppressed rebellion against a tetchy and censorious parent who so manifestly disliked change. To be fair, it has to be added that King George seemed also to be averse to trying to teach his son

Opposite *The Yorks leaving Bruton Street for the 1927 tour of Australia and New Zealand. They would not see their infant daughter for another six months.*

and heir anything of the daily work that a Sovereign had to do; and it was hardly surprising that the carefree cocktail-party David more than once complained that his father was 'eternally at war with the twentieth century'.

Bertie, the second son, the newly married Duke of York, was a different character. He shared at least some of his father's ideas about customs and duties, and in any case the Duke was now happily out of the family nest and thus had little risk of wordy conflict with his parents. Life had taken a fortunate turn for him, for he had a wife who suffused a domestic atmosphere of comfort and affection. He had an adored partner to share his public engagements. He marvelled at the way she sailed through public duties on her own.

Above all, the Duchess began to give to him the sympathy and help he so badly needed over the making of even a very short speech. It was agony for Bertie to say a few words before an audience of strangers, such was the small vocal impediment from which he suffered. The trouble – which nobody had ever tried to cure – lay in hesitations of speech, sudden stops in the middle of sentences, and the inability at that time to pronounce, for instance, the initial hard consonants of certain words (he had always to be careful to say 'Their Majesties' instead of 'King and Queen'). His wife now took to rehearsing him gently in the sentences he aimed to say, and the serenity of her presence at his side made him more relaxed when he was on his feet and speaking his piece. She refused to believe that his falterings were incurable. She it was who brought improvement.

Presently she persuaded him to consult an Australian expert in tackling speech defects, a therapist named Lionel Logue who was practising in Harley Street. Fortunately the Duke got on well with Mr. Logue as an individual. He was at ease with him and therefore put his very considerable determination into the exercises and responses to the specialist's treatment. Part of the Logue therapy was to get his patient to breathe in a new way, consciously making his diaphragm work when he talked. Signs of hopeful results began to show within weeks of beginning the new method. The uncertainty in the voice never left the Duke, but from this time onwards he was by no means always faltering. The exhilaration of his new life as a married man, with gloom and indecisiveness left behind, also helped. So did the travels upon which he and the Duchess embarked.

Above *The Duchess of York in
1928 inspecting the 1st Battalion
Irish Guards at Chelsea Barracks,
London. It was St. Patrick's
Day, and she later presented
sprigs of shamrock to all ranks.*

Right *London, 1926. The Duke
admires the infant Princess
Elizabeth in the arms of her
mother.*

Princess Elizabeth is circled by her proud parents and by the grandparents, King George V and Queen Mary on the left and the Earl and Countess of Strathmore on the right.

During the first winter of her marriage, the Duchess suffered from bronchitis, and so in the second winter, 1924–25, her husband obtained the King's blessing to take her for a few weeks on a private visit to East African countries. A few official engagements had to come into the programme, but for the most part the visit was devoted to camping, sightseeing trips in remote country areas, and big game hunting. The health and strength of both the travellers benefited from the safari. It was an immense change. They clearly enjoyed the rough tent life in reserves and forests, the encounters with tribal chiefs, and the treks and explorations of rivers, more than the occasional cushioned receptions and soft comforts of this or that government house.

Later in the year 1925, back in London, the Duchess was able to contemplate an exciting prospect for the following Spring. She was expecting her first child.

When first married, the Yorks had lived at White Lodge in Richmond Park, Queen Mary's childhood place; but it had proved an antique, isolated and chilly barrack of a home (probably just the place for bronchitis!), so they had moved out and were still looking for a place in London itself when the baby was due. So Lady Strathmore offered the parental Bruton Street house as the birthplace. It was there that at 3.40 a.m. on April 21, 1926, the infant arrived. The child was a girl, fair-haired and pink and perfect: Princess Elizabeth Alexandra Mary – E. A. M., the same initials as the delighted mother's.

The happiness of Bertie and Elizabeth was complete. They had a family. The event was 'so wonderful and so strange as well, that I could scarcely believe it', said the Duke. His father, King George, was specially glad too, for this was the first grandchild in

the male line. This was the girl who was to become one day a Sovereign Queen – though that was a destiny not then in any remotest imagination. Indeed, expectation was that as time went by she would move further back rather than forward in the line of succession to the crown. The baby Princess's grandfather was firmly on the throne; his heir, the child's Uncle David, the Prince of Wales, was still a young man and it was to be assumed that in due course he would marry and have children; and moreover there was reasonable prospect that this new child's own parents would have male children, taking precedence over girls.

Thus the birth of Princess Elizabeth aroused a mild friendly interest, but was scarcely hot news. The Press and the news bulletins read over the new 'wireless' logged the arrival happily, but top billing was being given to the industrial unrest which was brewing in Britain. The unprecedented General Strike of 1926 exploded a fortnight after the little Princess was born, and it swept babies and well nigh everything else from the newspaper pages.

Eventually the upsetting strike was settled and the nation resumed its normal business. But the Duke and Duchess of York had not settled down with their curly-headed Princess more than a few months before a special assignment disturbed their life in a big way. The King decided that Bertie should undergo a test of major duty overseas. This meant that the new parents had to set off on a tour round the world, lasting a full six months. The main ordeal for the Duke was the visit to New Zealand and Australia to perform the opening ceremonies of the Federal Parliament buildings in the new Australian capital, Canberra. But the almost unbearable part of the undertaking, for the Duchess

especially, was that the eight-months-old daughter was left at home in England, left without father and mother from January to June, 1927.

Viewed today, that separation seems harsh – even though grandfather George the Fifth no doubt did not mean it to be so. Such a long parting would not for a moment be accepted in the Royal Family now. The present Prince Charles and his Princess of Wales took the tiny Prince William with them, naturally and happily, when they went on their tour of Australia and New Zealand in 1983 – and that was an absence from the home base of only a few weeks. Five years later, the present Duchess of York (the Sarah Ferguson who married Prince Andrew, who received his dukedom on his wedding day) left her infant daughter Princess Beatrice in England, when the child was only a few weeks old, to be with her husband whilst Prince Andrew was on ceremonial duty during Royal Navy service in Australia. But she was back with the baby after a month's absence. That was in 1988. There was some criticism in tabloid newspapers which declared that the Duchess should not so soon have left the side of the cradle. (No doubt there would have been just as much journalistic censure if the newborn one *had* been part of the royal baggage on the Antipodean journeying.)

During the 1927 tour, the infant Princess Elizabeth in England was well cared for. Queen Mary, so often portrayed as a remote and austere figure, became an attentive grandmother, bestowing on the child, who went to stay at Buckingham Palace as well as at the Hertfordshire house, an affection beyond any

Above Two *little Princesses of York now. This was a 1931 garden party at Glamis. Elizabeth (the present Queen Elizabeth II) holds her mother's hand whilst the nanny wheels baby Margaret in her perambulator.*

Opposite, top *Parents and grandparents at Princess Elizabeth's christening on 29 May 1926. At the time no one imagined that this child, the present Queen, would occupy the Throne.*

Opposite, bottom *The royal couple at Maitland, Australia.*

interest she had exhibited when her own children were young.

Meanwhile the tour was a hard exercise for the then Duke of York. Although he had gained some confidence when on public appearance, he was still highly strung and nervous when the centre of attention on important ceremonial occasions. Long pauses were apt to punctuate embarrassingly the addresses he had to utter. And His Royal Highness knew that in the antipodes critical eyes would be upon him because he and his wife were following a dazzlingly successful visit by the Prince of Wales a few years earlier. The triumphs of the Prince Charming brother, who had not a great deal to do then but smile broadly and grace scores of social gatherings, were still glowing in the memories of many of the people who now watched a man who seemed to them, at first, a dutiful but disappointingly dissimilar 'second string'. But he tackled manfully the formal engagements during which he had to stand up and speak on behalf of his King-Emperor father. The consciousness that the Duchess was sitting

beside him with head held high and a steady smile on her face, not only calmed Bertie and helped him along but soothed and reassured those who listened. He began to grow in performance and stature. Even when Her Royal Highness caught a chill and for a few days did not appear with him, her influence was still there, enabling him to become better with his words. (She had always gone through the scripts with him beforehand!)

Challenges did not end even when the couple were travelling homewards. One in particular was of a rare kind. They were sailing without escort in the battle-cruiser HMS *Renown* when, in the Indian Ocean and a thousand miles from land, fire broke out in the ship's boiler room and flames spread rapidly until they were only a few feet away from the oil tanks. The whole vessel, half full of smoke, was in danger of inferno and explosion. At once, the Duke became an incisive naval officer. He went below to the seat of the fire to be with those who were fighting the outbreak and bringing out the casualties.

Elizabeth helped in her own way. She deliberately showed no sign of alarm even when decks became hot and the order to leave ship was about to be given. There would be no panic around *her*. She carried on as though she had hardly noticed the emergency. At length, to the relief of all, the fire was extinguished, just in time. The Yorks that night, instead of sitting in an open boat in the middle of a great sea, went thankfully to their beds. Afterwards, the *Renown*'s captain said to the Duchess: 'Did you realize, ma'am, that at one time it was pretty bad?' 'Yes, I did,' she replied. 'Every hour someone came to tell me that there was

43

Top *King George V in 1933 with the ladies of the family in front of the miniature Welsh Cottage, at Royal Lodge, Windsor.*

Bottom *A charming studio portrait of Queen Elizabeth and her two daughters. It was taken in December 1936, the month of the Abdication which was totally to alter the family's way of life.*

nothing to worry about – so I knew there was real trouble.'

When the travellers returned at last to London from their odyssey there were crowds cheering a welcome outside Buckingham Palace; and, best of all, a fourteen-months-old Princess was waving from the parapet of the Palace's central balcony which faces the Mall. A little later, united with her parents, the child was also held up to wave from another but nearby balcony, a new one, belonging to a tall, terraced house simply called '145 Piccadilly'. It was at the Hyde Park end of the famous street. This was the house (demolished in the 1950s) which had been found for the Yorks and in which they lived for the next decade. They had a real family home at last. The Duchess made the place a domestic haven, bright, airy, comfortable, with a top floor nursery where the small daughter was cherished but by no means spoilt. All those inside 'Number 145' enjoyed a reasonable privacy like any other upper-class family, with no sentries or police guards at the door. It was characteristic of the Duchess's aversion to fussy protocol that nothing whatever denoted the fact that this was a residence of royalty.

But people began to know about the popular family whose house it was. From family friends and from some of the staff, pretty stories about the Princess circulated, injecting charm into the frenzied Twenties and Thirties. She was known, they said, as 'Lilibet', which was her first attempt at saying her own name – and it is a fact that the childish invention has endured: her own folk use it to this day. Less firmly based on fact, though believed to be only slightly embroidered, are the anecdotes that she called George the Fifth 'Grandpapa England', and that, hearing carols at Sandringham one Christmas, particularly the song about 'Glad tidings of great joy I bring to you and all mankind', she piped: 'I know Old Man Kind: it's Grandpapa'.

Old Man Kind, a few years after the Yorks were established in the Piccadilly house, gave to them, as a grace-and-favour residence out of town, the house which remains to this day the loved week-end retreat of the Queen Mother – Royal Lodge, Windsor, situated in the private south-eastern corner of the Great Park, half way between Windsor Castle and Virginia Water. Bertie and Elizabeth, equal in their keenness to possess a good retreat of their own to cultivate, jumped at the chance of a quiet country home. They soon began to carve out woodland gardens around the then-dilapidated house, whose history had begun very many years before even its notable occupation by the Prince Regent, the future George IV. Royally appointed 'Rangers' of the Park once lived there or had covetous eyes on it – and these included George II's third son, the soldier Duke of Cumberland who was notorious for his brutal repression of the Highlanders in the middle of the eighteenth century (which did not prevent Elizabeth Bowes-Lyon, for all her Scottish Jacobite partiality, from being attracted to the place!) The Lodge had suffered numerous ornate conversions and rebuildings, and both Nash and Wyatville had a hand in some of the alterations.

In modern history, the Lodge's greatest importance – certainly in the Queen Mother's eyes – is in the fact that she and her husband, before they became King and Queen, and later too, revelled in a personal creating of the house's lovely grounds as they are today: acres of delight, winding paths and clean rides through the woods, and beds of shrubs and flowers garlanding the dwelling. The Duke and Duchess of York, as they were in those days, literally became the Lodge's head gardeners.

The royal work parties in those grounds during the early

nineteen-thirties must have made amusing pictures. Whenever possible on Saturdays and Sundays Their Royal Highnesses would go down to the Lodge, taking cold lunches and old clothes with them. In the early stages of attacking the wilderness, the gardening was mainly a business of bush-clearing, hacking through thickets, making bonfires of old wood from lopped trees, and putting in plants whilst foundations of lawns and patios were being laid. Battle orders were issued by the Duke, axes, saws and pruning bills brought out, and all hands pressed into service.

Queen Elizabeth recalls afternoons when visitors, perhaps calling for tea, were conscripted to join the hard-labouring gangs in which, indistinguishable one from another, there worked princess and secretary, duke and valet, equerry and chauffeur, butler and policeman, all covered in dirt and twigs as they hacked and crawled through tangled thickets together. On one Saturday a huge Guards officer became part of the gang. Wanting to get used to his black bearskin cap – it was a new one and would have to be worn at a parade on the following week – he deliberately kept the headgear on whilst acting as wheelbarrow-boy for the Duke. As the afternoon became hotter and hotter he toiled on, stripped himself to the waist, covered his middle with nothing but an old pair of khaki shorts, but retained his towering furry headgear firmly strapped. 'In full dress – but only down to his brow', remarked the Duchess.

It was not at the Lodge, nor in London, but back at her old home, Glamis Castle, that in 1930 Elizabeth gave birth to her second child, another daughter. Princess Margaret Rose (whom her parents wished to call Anne, but that name was vetoed by the old King) emerged on a night of thunder and howling gale:

August 21. She was the first member of the Royal Family to be born in Scotland for well over three hundred years. And the baby Margaret gave much joy, born though she was into a Britain still gripped by troubles in industry and characterized by the Hunger Marches.

The two little girls were brought up together, educated at home by nurses, governesses and later by various specialist tutors; and gradually they began to be seen in public. In 1934 Princess Elizabeth was a bridesmaid at the wedding of the beautiful Princess Marina of Greece to the spirited and good looking Prince George, Duke of Kent, who was Bertie's youngest brother (though nearest to eldest son David in character). A year later came the autumn marriage of the slightly older brother, Prince Henry, Duke of Gloucester, to Lady Alice Montagu-Douglas-Scott, daughter of the Scottish peer, the Duke of Buccleuch.

Earlier in 1935 both the little Princesses attended the thanksgiving service in St. Paul's Cathedral which marked the Silver Jubilee of the grandparents King George and Queen Mary.

Those Thirties were years during which the dark shadows of the dictators were beginning to edge across Europe and into British anxieties. Adolf Hitler, as new German chancellor, god of the Nazis and despot of his militarized country, was beginning the brutal expansion of the Reich; the Italians were about to invade Abyssinia, the country that is now Ethiopia; and Spain

Pets and family on the lawn at the Royal Lodge, Windsor, in 1936.

Opposite *The royal couple with Princess Elizabeth and a corgi on the steps of 145 Piccadilly, their London home, before they moved, as King and Queen, to Buckingham Palace.*

Above *The very elegantly dressed Royal Highness – Duchess of York when this photograph was taken – on the garden terrace of Buckingham Palace.* ·

was on the brink of civil war. Strife on a global scale was looming: World War Two.

But several years before 1939 a worry of an intimate and very personal kind was hovering near Britain's Royal Family. It was only a thin cloud at first, and not thought likely to have any wide consequences: a matter causing a few frowns and eyebrow raisings, but no more. Yet it was something which was destined to swell into a national cataclysm. The cloud came from the still-unmarried David, the eldest brother, Prince of Wales and Heir to the Throne, the brightest figure of them all in the eyes of the world.

He was the one who, before long, was to shake the monarchy, appal the Yorks and revolutionize their lives – and spring Elizabeth Bowes-Lyon to an unsought stardom.

The Prince of Wales had experienced a frustrating time in the *First* World War. Though then a very young man, he had been in khaki and had always been eager for action; he had not, however, been allowed to be in the front-line trenches during any of the great battles. He would probably have been killed. After the war was over, unsettled and unsatisfied like many of his generation who luckily survived, he plunged vigorously into the variegated Society of the gay Twenties, hunting in very mixed company, feverishly party-going in a whirl of lively ladies and

late nights. To the outside world, during travels on whatever royal flag-waving missions were given him, he was a sporting Beau Ideal, his superficial graces and good looks quite devastating. He made some spasmodic efforts to take a real interest in social problems, miners' welfare, foreign trade. To his brothers and sister, certainly to the Duke of York and his Duchess, he was for the most part a relative of charm and kindness on the occasions when they met. He was affectionate, certainly impressionable. But also – and this was something which began the family's worry – he became increasingly self-centred and inconsiderate. He was immature. He was, understandably, in revolt against the Victorian code of behaviour which still ruled in the house of George the Fifth, his father.

Victim, without doubt, of a generation gap.

That world of brother-in-law David and his brassy new-found friends was not Elizabeth's world; it knew nothing of serene domesticity. He and she met happily enough on royal duty and at gatherings of the clan. But then they went their different ways, he to his night-clubs and she to a loved home and happy husband and children which were the 'matchless blessing' that David as a departing monarch was publicly to envy in the famous Abdication broadcast of farewell and handover at the end of 1936.

As the Prince of Wales pursued his own pleasure-seeking way through the Thirties, and stood smiling dutifully upon his brothers when they married, it was clear that he himself was far from 'settling down' as his father prayed he would do. Family and nation looked forward hopefully to a Prince of Wales wedding, yet nothing came. Liaisons, yes; nuptials, no.

But he had met in London the woman who was to prove the one consuming love of his life and for whom, later, he would quit inherited kingship to go abroad and, shunned, marry his choice and enter a long night of self-imposed banishment.

That lay in the future. In the mid-Thirties, when the association with the then Mrs. Wallis Warfield Simpson was growing, the public knew nothing of it. But in the Royal Family reluctant notice had to be taken of David's consuming devotion to the smart lady from America, already once divorced. The brightly entertaining new socialite who talked with an ingratiating Baltimore drawl fascinated the Prince as no other woman had done. In the company of her and her friends, he drew more and more away from his family. Old King George, horrified but helpless, growled: 'The boy will ruin himself in twelve months after I'm gone.'

The precarious state of George the Fifth's health after he had rallied from the illnesses of 1928 and 1931 was another secret kept from public knowledge. The Duchess of York knew it well and made as much fuss of her father-in-law as his nature allowed her to do. She had discerned the King's simple honesty, kindness, and vulnerability too, which lay behind the sometimes unprepossessing exterior. He had no genius – and no conceit. When he and Queen Mary celebrated that Silver Jubilee on May 6, 1935, the welcome they received when driving through the streets of London astonished and moved him. At home in the Palace that night, whilst beacons burned and the nation still celebrated, he wrote in his diary: 'They must really like me.'

He had enjoyed his day. They all had. In another carriage of the royal procession rode the Yorks, accompanied now by their two girls, Princess Elizabeth (nine years old) and Princess Margaret (four). It was a day remembered by the elder daughter when, forty-two years later, she was a Sovereign herself and rode through even greater waves of affection on *her* Silver Jubilee.

But in 1935 Grandpapa was a sick man, his mind as racked by the menacing march of Brown Shirt troops in Germany as his body was by the conquering bronchitis. The Europe he knew was dying, and so was he. When his family gathered for that year's Christmas at Sandringham he was failing fast; he lasted only until January 20, 1936 (just before Hitler occupied the Rhineland), and the ending of his reign was broadcast in one of the most apposite sentences of BBC bulletins: 'The King's life is moving peacefully to its close.'

Peace for him, but not for the world. Nor for the family he had left. Events to come were dramatically beyond any forecasting – certainly beyond the imagining of the family at 145 Piccadilly, where 'Bertie' the head of the household was, because of his brother's accession as monarch, the immediate next in the line of Succession. He had become Heir Presumptive. But that, it was reasonably assumed, was only a temporary situation. The new king was 41 years old. Sometime – probably before long, the public thought – he would marry and have children who in the fullness of time would succeed him. To the Duchess of York the hope and belief must have been that her husband was indeed merely the Heir *Provisional* – just for the time being.

Top *The fashionable Duchess walks through old Brussels during 'British Week' at the International Exhibition in July 1935.*

Bottom *King George VI taking the salute at a distribution of medals to Overseas Contingents at Buckingham Palace two days after the Coronation. Behind him are Queen Elizabeth, Queen Mary, the Princesses Elizabeth and Margaret, and the Duchess of Gloucester.*

Opposite *The royal couple in Bethnal Green, London, in 1929. Fashions were beginning to change.*

H.R.H THE PRINCE OF WALES.

Top *Smiling 'David', when Prince of Wales, was immensely popular, and picture postcards of him proliferated. (There were fewer smiles when he briefly became King Edward VIII.)*

Bottom *In the twilight years. Here he is Duke of Windsor, pictured almost two decades after the Abdication. With his Duchess, he was on a visit to England.*

So, a new reign. A time for excitement, and not immediate anxiety, as to the Throne came David, no longer Prince of Wales but His Majesty King Edward the Eighth. Still the Golden Boy, cynosure of great expectations and goodwill, focus of the ideals of a post-war generation. It was felt that kingship would now move with the times and that this vigorous monarch would rise to the responsibilities of his office, even though perhaps it would, to him, mean a great change in a way of life so characterized by swinging informality. The loyalty and devotion of the rest of the Royal Family was without question at his feet. Here was a man who could use his popularity to bring closer together the work of the Palace and the work of the people beyond its walls. Gaps between eras and between classes could be bridged by a man like David. That is what was widely expected.

But the hopes never came to fulfilment. What the new king seemed not to comprehend was that life was no longer a matter of cheery waves, emotive beaming, and off to the next frolic. Much more than bright appearances, and the image of an open-air sportsman, was needed now. In the past he had performed public service of minor kinds, and certainly had made himself loved, but now he had to *work* at being a monarch. Good intentions, boyish enthusiasms, these were not enough. Soon it was plain to members of the Family – as it was at a very late stage to the public – that although Edward VIII began by making some slapdash attempts seriously to tackle the tasks of Head of State, he was not able to reconcile what had become a self-indulgent private life with the duties of a constitutional Sovereign. As time went by, his failings told. Often impatient and manifestly unstable, shallow and selfish, he was in any case too easily discouraged if some small impulsive change made by him did not turn out right. He resented criticism, often was inconsiderate in rejecting advice which was fairly based on tradition and experience. As a king, David was now seen as a man impulsive without being inspired. He was strong in charm but weak in talent.

Even in the first few months of that 1936 reign he was beginning to spend more time on house parties and holidays than on perusing State documents and performing public ceremonies. Loathing stuffiness, ever anxious to rush his fences, reforming all too brusquely the protocol and patterns of his father's court, he caused dismay and offence by sudden and thoughtless staff changes. Inescapable duties irked him. Understandably, the old Establishment had to campaign against his ways and against neglects which sometimes impeded processes of government.

Most worrying to his Family was that they, as well as his Palace desk, were being neglected as a consequence of his attachment to Mrs. Simpson. His desire for her company became all-engrossing. He was obsessively in love, his mind set upon a future with her beside him, notwithstanding the differences in their circumstances and stations. Soon she was with him almost everywhere, cruising abroad and even staying at Sandringham and Balmoral, at first as guest but later making appearances in the role of hostess, bright with the jewels which were his gifts.

It was shocking to the Duke and Duchess of York, straining to understand and forgive though they were. They were saddened by the change in David towards themselves. They hardly ever saw him. Once so affectionate and close, he was now difficult to get hold of, even on the telephone. Glimpses of him were of a person becoming irritable and evasive. He hated Buckingham

Top *Edward VIII in 1936, the one year of his reign.*

Bottom *In November 1936 King Edward VIII visited the mining district of South Wales. Here he is accompanied by Ernest Brown, then Minister of Labour (on his left) and Sir Kingsley Wood.*

INSTRUMENT OF ABDICATION

I, Edward the Eighth, of Great
Britain, Ireland, and the British Dominions
beyond the Seas, King, Emperor of India, do
hereby declare My irrevocable determination
to renounce the Throne for Myself and for
My descendants, and My desire that effect
should be given to this Instrument of
Abdication immediately.

In token whereof I have hereunto set
My hand this tenth day of December, nineteen
hundred and thirty six, in the presence of
the witnesses whose signatures are subscribed.

SIGNED AT
FORT BELVEDERE
IN THE PRESENCE
OF

Edward RI

Albert

Henry.

George.

Palace: happiness was Fort Belvedere, a castellated folly near Virginia Water, which he had made his favourite and private house. There he flung himself into rough and ready gardening, derisively playing bagpipes whilst marching through the bushes – an odd indulgence for him – and entertaining an assortment of friends on long week-ends. No more was he the Uncle David who would pop in to Number 145 to see the two Princesses and their parents. The one person who absorbed his interest was Wallis Simpson (soon to divorce Husband Number Two). The King

Above Abdication. The historic document of 1936, issued by a departing Edward VIII. It is witnessed by his three royal brothers.

Opposite An aerial view of Fort Belvedere, the house loved and lived in by the Royal Family's David in '36 whilst he was King (he disliked palaces). 'The Fort' is situated near Virginia Water, at the far south of Windsor Great Park.

was determined to make her his wife, even if it meant giving up the Crown.

But the lady, a divorcée, could not be accepted by Britain or the Empire and Commonwealth as Queen or as the wife of a reigning King – moreover, Edward VIII was head of a Church of England one of whose principles was that Christian marriage was indissoluble. A constitutional crisis developed and deepened, jarring many hopes and sympathies too – for a desire for the Monarch's happiness was widespread. It became clear to those 'in the know' that he was going to follow the dictates of his heart, even though renouncing his office would explode a bomb in Britain. In the circumstances, he saw no other choice but to give up the Throne. The idea that Stanley Baldwin was the villain of the piece was false: the Prime Minister was not essentially at odds with his Sovereign. Prime Minister and King, both of them, each along his path, wished *not* to divide the country. Winston Churchill it was who might have formed a useless 'King's Party', for Mr. Churchill, royalist and romantic, was dismayed at the thought of forcing out a monarch. For a while, misjudging the feelings of Parliament and a majority of the people, he tried to rally support for a compromise or temporary move to delay a fateful departure. But the public, when the full facts were presented, were sorrowfully at one with the steady and firm decisions of both Home and Dominion ministers against any such thing as a morganatic marriage. An inexorable tide was against Edward VIII.

He had to go.

The abdication was virtually a settled thing before most people in Britain were aware that the scarcely-gossiped 'royal love affair' was in fact a major constitutional crisis and a danger to the Crown. For although through many weeks and months of 1936 the newspapers and magazines of half the world had been featuring the 'romance' of the British King and Wallis Simpson, the Press and the B.B.C. at home had hardly mentioned it. (Today, half a century later, the climate of opinion and of morals, and the business of news reporting, is utterly different; most of those who practise in what is today termed the Media – and who hold almost nothing to be sacred or secret – have hard work to believe the reticence of fifty years ago.)

Only on December 1 – on the odd excuse that a bishop (who in fact had scarcely heard of Mrs. Simpson) had made a little speech in which he hoped that the King could be a regular

CHAPTER FIVE

VALIANT CONSORT

To say that the year 1936 was phenomenal is understatement. Britain had three successive kings on its Throne within a twelvemonth. The second one, Edward the Eighth, poised as the most attractive monarch of the century though he had once seemed, proved to be the most awkward and unfit one, so that his departure from office after only 325 days can be seen as a blessing in disguise, the best thing that could have happened to the monarchy. His place was taken by a man of self-sacrifice and resolve, a prince who proved to be an embodiment of the enduring virtues of his country: George the Sixth.

The truth of the change was not immediately to be seen. Nor, at the time, was the burden that had been thrust upon the wife who was now a Queen. The abdication crisis was an appalling shock to the Duchess of York, its trauma all the greater because of her husband's immeasurable dismay at taking his brother's place. Elizabeth had met Mrs. Simpson, found her quite alien to her own way of life. She was horrified that David was so infatuated by the lady. At the beginning of the affair she was upset – as much as stately Queen Mary was – but it was not her way to contemplate or anticipate unpleasant possibilities. She and Bertie had not tried to influence David over the lady of his choice any more than they had over his irresponsibility as Head of State. She knew David was wayward and rash; she cannot but have disliked the idea of the American as her prospective sister-in-law. To many people Mrs. Simpson was very dislikeable indeed, and condemnations were spoken loud. But no evidence has been produced that Elizabeth gave public utterance to private feelings; nor has anything been adduced that she was instigator of the subsequent boycott of the Windsors. Queen Mary's implacable hostility to Wallis was at the heart of that.

Only in the last frenetic days of David's tenure of office as a king did Elizabeth, in consternation not helped by a severe bout of influenza, accept what had become inevitable and bring her iron-willed calmness to bear upon the fact that she and the Duke were about to be precipitated into a frighteningly different life: King and Queen.

Opposite *Queen Elizabeth and Queen Mary with the two Princesses (a Guide and a Brownie) in the Quadrangle of Windsor Castle during a Girl Guide Rally at Windsor in 1938*

She had no illusions, no hesitations either, about the task once it was forced upon them. A frightening task. But she was sustained by the conviction that her husband, distressed and unrehearsed though he was, would not shrink or spare himself. With her help.

December 11, 1936 was the date on which Albert, Duke of York, became King George VI, three days before his forty-first birthday. His wife, the Lady Elizabeth Bowes-Lyon of only a dozen years before, was thus Queen Consort and Empress at the age of thirty-six. Gone was the cosy house in Piccadilly: her home was now the vast headquarters of the constitutional monarchy, Buckingham Palace with its six hundred rooms, the whole great place full of bewildering, echoing chambers whose heating and lighting and plumbing had been antique for years. This was the family establishment now, this the workshop from which King and Queen together gradually rebuilt the monarchy which the surrender of his post by David might have wrecked. History proved that, on the contrary, the Throne, though it might momentarily have shivered, was not destroyed, but steadily became firm and strong after the departure of the iconoclast king. His replacement was, as it turned out, an eventually effective Sovereign, a gentle and sensible progressive, a man whose transparent goodness and staunchness became a loved national asset. The Crown was esteemed as it had not been for years.

How did the hesitant Bertie manage this miracle? The answer is that he did not – not by himself. The achievement was as much to the credit of the new Queen Consort as to him. She was an incomparable support, her optimism and good sense were at her husband's service daily, steadying his nerves, helping him to have an undreamed-of confidence that he *could* answer the calls of high office. He listened to advice but when he took decisions they were wise and his own.

Nevertheless, it was undoubtably team work by a man and his wife that restored the situation at Buckingham Palace. No monarch ever stood less alone than George VI, none so endowed with a vivifying partner. She underpinned all his reconstruction. Many ministers he had, but his Consort was his surest mainstay.

Not that he was a weak king: only inexperienced at first. It was simply that the character of Queen Elizabeth, and the example of loyalty and family unity which she presented to him and to the

world did wonders to strengthen the Throne. It might well have been impossible in 1936 and 1937 for the newcomer to tackle kingship at all without such a woman beside him. As it was, a good king became a great one; and Bertie and Elizabeth brought British monarchy back to respect and then to regard.

It was indeed 'Us – together'.

And what a huge but neglected house the new Queen Consort suddenly had to run! The Palace was a complicated domain, and the family which now moved into it had to experience all around them a *State* household as well as, and vastly bigger than, their own domestic one. There were stiff hierarchies Downstairs as well as Upstairs. The staff were numbered in hundreds: chefs and footmen, grooms and porters, secretaries and surveyors, specialists all in high or low degree, from Master of the Household to maids and apprentice cleaners serving such personages as the Page of the Back Stairs and the Chief Yeoman of the Glass and China Pantry.

The First Lady was soon sorting them out, smoothing feathers which had been ruffled, and seeing the departments smoothly about their business, whether the business was the visit of a viceroy or the vagaries of a vacuum cleaner. It did not take Queen Elizabeth long to make the private apartments homely as they had never been. Comfortable furniture was moved in from

145 Piccadilly; and a warmth of family character began to transform the Palace's huge rooms as the filled bookcases, gramophones and records, pianos, easy chairs, bright pictures, sensible tables and vases for abundances of flowers arrived.

It was soon after this time, when national responsibilities and public appearances were increasingly taken and made, that Her Majesty was noticed, especially by the fashion-conscious, to be presenting a maturely sophisticated and markedly attractive figure in her manner of dressing. The eye-catching hats and brightly tasteful gowns appeared, the light furs and the pearl necklaces, and especially the varieties of pastel colours which marked her ensembles. More sophisticated hairstyles replaced the fringe. The beautifully dressed Queen, to be an admired part of the British scene for a long time to come, was starting to emerge.

The new reign – with a king who named himself after his father and was clearly following that bearded paterfamilias in personal integrity and in respecting the traditional standards of behaviour which had belonged to George V's years – had its greatest ceremonial occasion in the Spring of 1937: the Coronation, an ordeal in itself. Sovereign and Consort on golden thrones together – for she too was crowned. The ancient rite in Westminster Abbey came upon them more quickly than is usual

Opposite *When the* Empress of Britain *docked at Southampton, bringing Their Majesties home from their visit to Canada and the United States, the two Princesses boarded the liner to greet their parents. Here two small page boys present giant pandas to the Princesses on behalf of the crew.*

Right *The King and Queen inspect a child's book during a visit to the Elementary School section of the Royal Agricultural Society's Centenary Show in Windsor Great Park in July 1939.*

at the beginning of a reign: long planning and preparation are needed, and normally well over a year separates Coronation from Accession. For this new King and Queen only five months had elapsed, because they adhered to the date that had been fixed for the crowning of the brother who never reached it (souvenirs for him had already been made and marketed: Edward VIII coronation mugs, inscribed with an untruth, are collectors' items).

Queen Elizabeth took a personal hand in much of the Coronation preliminaries and rehearsals, not least in helping Mr. Logue in schooling the King in the ordained responses he would have to make in the church.

May 12 was the date. Rainstorms did not seem to dim the pageantry or deter the London crowds. On this occasion the service in the Abbey *was* broadcast on the wireless: sound-radio and its microphones, yes, but no such thing as a television camera was allowed in. There was filming, however; and in the clamorous streets outside, the processions were stars of the first-ever 'live' TV outside-broadcast – moving pictures transmitted directly to viewers by the B.B.C., whose public high-definition television service, the first in the world, had started six months before.

Inside the Abbey, the whole Royal Family was assembled – from Queen Mary, now Queen Dowager, to those two small Princesses who were her grandchildren. Elizabeth was just eleven years old, Margaret six-and-a-half. They had been excitedly awake and up half the night, at the Palace, peeping through windows and listening to marching feet and the testing of street loud-speakers. As a result, Margaret had a struggle to keep awake as she, with the others, watched the long ceremony from the Royal Gallery of an Abbey packed almost to the roof by a vast congregation.

The King got through the taxing ritual remarkably well, rising to the challenge of a series of *contretemps* which, in the event, probably helped him to overcome his nervousness. The Dean at one point tried to put a white surplice on His Majesty inside-out, and had to be corrected; the Archbishop, holding up the Form of Service for the King to speak, covered with his thumb the very words of the Oath; the Lord Great Chamberlain fumbled so much over buckling-on the Sovereign's vestments that the King had to fix a sword-belt himself; and there was clerical uncertainty and much twisting-about before they got the St. Edward's Crown, weighing seven pounds, the right way round on the royal brow. Worse still, the King was caused to stumble and nearly fall down when a bishop trod on the royal robe – and had to be told, with the sharpness of a naval command, to get off the thing.

The Queen watched him with anxiety but with loving pride. However tense within, she was externally calm. You might have thought she did this sort of thing *every* Wednesday afternoon. Yet it was with inborn faith and dedication that she sailed through the whole ritual, smilingly confident, a picture of gracefulness when her turn came to kneel and be blessed and anointed beneath a canopy held aloft by four duchesses. She was crowned with a new crown, probably the prettiest and most precious of all, made for her of platinum and gold, and finely jewelled. The principal diamond sparkling in it was the famous Koh-i-Noor ('Mountain of Light') which had been presented to Queen Victoria by the East India Company in 1849 on the annexation of the Punjab.

The Coronation was a high point of ceremonial history and a

A pensive moment, during the Royal Family's visit to Edinburgh in July 1947.

fine piece of pageantry, but, to the two who were at its centre, i was above all an event of spiritual significance, an ac betokening religious faith and duty. As a spectacle, sadly it wa destined to be the last bright gleam in a twilight of peace.

On the Eve of War
King and Queen were now deep in the public engagements o State. Deep too in the mounting anxieties of an ominou international situation. Clearly, it seemed, European conflic was once more imminent, and Britain inescapably involved Fear was in all hearts as the next year came. The Continent la under totalitarian threat from the conquering Nazis, nov annexing territories in their march to war, which was stayed only briefly by Neville Chamberlain's flying visit to Germany The Prime Minister came back waving a piece of paper from Hitler – a document of the British politician's Munich Surrender, so it very soon proved. He had bought only a little time: 1938 was a dolorous year.

It was also a year of personal sadness for the Queen, for Lad Strathmore, the dear and gifted mother, died, at the age of 75 and was buried at Glamis. (Her father lived for another six years he died in 1944, aged 89.) Family mourning for the Countes postponed a state visit to France, but in July 1938 the King and Queen did go to Paris, and the visit – whether it helped th *Entente Cordiale* or not – was a personal success. Spectacula parades studded the four-day programme; the streets of th

Gallic capital crowed delight; but what took the greatest attention of the French public and its Press was the stunning *trousseau* of the British Queen. Norman Hartnell's many years of designing and dressmaking for Her Majesty were beginning, with great effect. Months before, he had devised flowing dresses of brilliant colours; and now, in three weeks after the Queen's bereavement, and only a few hours before Their Majesties sailed for France, he and his workrooms entirely remade some thirty dresses – in a royal *white* of mourning. The crinoline-style gowns which were the sensation of that State visit were inspired by the Winterhalter portraits of the young Queen Victoria which the King had shown Hartnell on a visit to the picture gallery at Buckingham Palace.

When the royal party returned from Paris it was a return to scenes of grim reality in the face of the advancing storm from Europe. Trenches were being dug in the London parks as refuges from air raiders; gasmasks were being issued – to Palace people like everybody else; the Fleet was mobilized; and first steps were taken for the transport of children who were about to be evacuated from the cities. Britain was on the brink of war.

Long before, it had been arranged that, at the end of September, the King should go to Clydebank to launch the world's largest liner which was to bear his wife's name; but when the time came, the crisis kept him in London and the Queen travelled north to perform the ceremony in his stead. It was on the next day that Mr. Chamberlain, with sudden hope, made that rush to Nazi Bavaria and returned with Hitler's Anglo-German 'friendship pact' which in the relief of the moment was hailed as token of peace. But the Munich 'Agreement' was appeasement which staved off an inevitable outbreak of war for a bare twelve months only.

Then came 1939 and its ominous summer. Though the world was on the edge of catastrophe, Sovereign and Consort made a crossing to the other side of the Atlantic: on the face of it, a strange and hazardous absence from home. But it was on advice that they undertook that long-planned visit to Canada and the United States. There was urgent need for Britain to be strengthening friendships, and this King and Queen had already been seen as the best ambassadors the country had. So it was a six weeks' slog that they tackled, with nothing in the long days' programmes shirked, coast to coast across the North American continent. A spectacular and memorable success in which the impact of Queen Elizabeth was paramount. Both as a person and as a representative, the impression she made is part of eve-of-war history. She in effect helped to rebuild Anglo-US understanding at a time of strain, for numbers of Americans then were, to say the least of it, neutral and isolationist in their attitude to Europe's peril: Hitler and Mussolini were not *their* problem. That was what many felt – *Before they Met The Lady.*

And something more, too, came from her contacts and conversations. Being a realist – and a good and true reporter – she, whilst not airing any private views over recent events in the Royal Family, did much to dispel misapprehensions on the other side of the Atlantic, where there was belief that Britain was a hotbed of anti-American sentiments and that the real reason for the 'dismissal' of Edward VIII was the Duchess of Windsor's nationality.

The very sight of the Queen gave pleasure, as did her manner. 'Just what royal ladies *should* look like', was often heard and read. 'Just how we like Top Folks to be, whatever side of the tracks they're on.' During the long journeys across the continent, she

A garden party at Port Elizabeth during the South African tour of 1947.

and the King took full advantage of halts, even short ones. Day after day they would leave the royal train and, to the consternation of the security men, plunge into the crowds and talk. (These were the first 'walkabouts', many years before the Australian word was taken up and overworked by today's journalists to describe the *Second* Elizabeth's excursions.) Quebec specially loved the lady, applauded her polished French accent. Press photographers in every province discovered that she too had a news-picture sense: she paused naturally where they'd hoped she would, so they got good shots with the light right and both the setting and the now-famous smile shining.

Slowly, as the train crossed vast plains and rumbled through the Rockies, the goodwill spread: interest escalated in the provincial capitals but in the smaller communities as well. The verdict was that these two people from the Old Country were 'really O.K.'. They weren't show-offs and weren't putting on an act. So they were remembered – just as the travellers themselves remembered the people and the places where people had waited to wave: places with names like Moose Jaw, Medicine Hat, Sioux Lookout or Kicking Horse Pass. Often, groups of Canadian countryfolk who had ridden far stood at the tracksides for hours, just to see the train go by.

Queen Elizabeth gave instructions that the King and she must be told whenever the engineer observed a collection of people by the side of the line ahead, so that *they* could be seen waving back from a window. 'Slow down, so that we all get a good look', she said.

Historic moments of the Coronation on May 12, 1937, showing the new King George VI in the Coronation Chair in Westminster Abbey (above); Sovereign and Consort, crowned King and Queen, at London's Admiralty Arch during the long Coronation Day procession in the Golden Coach (opposite, top); not only her husband, but Queen *Elizabeth too was crowned during the glittering ceremony in the Abbey (opposite, bottom).*

*A picture taken immediately after the Coronation of King George VI on
14 May 1937. The King and Queen Elizabeth are wearing their
Coronation robes and crowns. In regalia too are the Princesses, eleven-
year-old Elizabeth and six-year-old Margaret.*

The King and Queen on the balcony of Buckingham Palace with Princess Elizabeth, Princess Margaret and their attendants. They had just returned from the Crowning in the Abbey.

One time, late at night, word came back on the telephone from the driver's cab of expectation that they'd be passing an unusually large assembly of people on horseback a few miles ahead. The Queen got up, wrapped a warm dressing-gown round her, did her hair and put one of her tiaras on. She was seen, well lighted and waving both hands, on the royal coach's observation-platform as the train went at snail's pace through the cheering and lamp-waving night riders. (She was never one to disappoint a gathering. The present writer remembers her, one sweltering African morning during another tour, dressing up in jewels and full evening gown at 10 a.m. to appear at a Zulu assembly – 'because that is how they would expect me to look, and I wouldn't want them to think it isn't me'.)

The King and Queen, on that 1939 tour, were the first reigning Sovereign and Consort to set foot on American soil. President Roosevelt and his wife were their hosts during the days in the U.S.A.; and the welcomes were astonishing. In the capital half a million people packed Pennsylvania Avenue, and newspaper headlines blazed: 'The British re-capture Washington'. In New York, crowds at the World's Fair yelled 'Attaboy, Queen!'

Elizabeth's impact on the transatlantic scene had something like the effect one of her granddaughters-by-marriage had half a century later – though the thousands who then jostled to glimpse Diana, Princess of Wales, told largely of a younger generation's frenzied curiosity which centred on the glamorous much-photographed fashion-plate figure of the girl who had married the Heir to the Second Elizabeth. In 1939, though sometimes there was hysteria in the crowds, the salute was to a known human being, fine clothes or not. People were hailing a manifestly stalwart leading lady on the world's stage. Elizabeth's sheer personality was what captivated.

As Hitler loomed on the other side of the ocean, it was certainly this royal lady who played a significant part in turning the tide of America's affection and aid towards Britain. That North American journey during May and June was a job well done, a worthwhile experience, during which royal popularity had led unmistakably to political advantage. A tour to remember – and a *tour de force*.

The return of the travellers to the United Kingdom was met by a display of public affection beyond anything expected. Reports of the tour had been flooding back, showing that it had been a perfect winner, the antithesis of the perfunctory plod through lukewarm prairies which some critics had predicted. Politicians in particular understood clearly that they had acquired an appealing King and Queen, to whom American experience had given professional assurance.

On the brink of world tragedy though we were – indeed partly *because* we were – men and women turned gratefully to this royal couple who were already becoming a focus of national identity and purpose. Established in their own right now, they were to win the further pride of a nation in combat during the five years to come.

Just one other agreeable event, which was to have a profound effect on the Family's personal future, took place in that last summer of peace, 1939. The King and Queen took their two daughters with them on a visit to the Royal Naval College at Dartmouth in Devon. Their kinsman Lord Mountbatten had arranged for Cadet Captain Philip Mountbatten, Prince Philip of Greece, to look after the visitors; and there it was that the thirteen-years-old Princess Elizabeth met and talked for a whole day with Uncle Dickie's young nephew. It has always been said that from that day there was, for the Princess, 'no one else'. Her heart was Philip's – all through the war that followed.

Left *An Indian child greets the King and Queen in the tribe's encampment at Calgary, Alberta, in July 1939 during the successful Canadian tour.*

Below *On the porch of Hyde Park, the Roosevelt home on the Hudson River, the King and Queen chat with the President, Franklin D. Roosevelt, his wife and mother.*

Opposite, top *King George VI making a radio broadcast from the Governor's house in Winnipeg, Manitoba, on Empire Day 1939, during the Royal Tour of Canada.*

Opposite, bottom *An historic meeting. Thirteen-year-old Princess Elizabeth visits Dartmouth College with her parents and sister on 22 July 1939 and is photographed for probably the first time with the young naval cadet destined to become her husband. Standing next to the uniformed Philip is his uncle and mentor, Lord Mountbatten.*

CHAPTER SIX

THROUGH WORLD WAR

COMMITTED to friends and allies, and aware that the dictators' trampling course had to be contested in the cause of civilized freedom and sheer national survival, Britain took inescapable resort to arms at the end of that 1939 summer. Nazi aggression had gobbled Austria, and much more. When German forces ignored warnings and invaded Poland on the first day of September, full mobilization in the United Kingdom was executed at once; and, as Warsaw burned, a state of hostility against Germany was declared on September 3. The Second World War had begun.

Memories of those darkening days are dimming now, fifty years later, though enduring words such as 'blackout' and 'blitz' and 'battle-dress' do not have to be explained. Many families still recall the pictures of troop-trains and the first British soldiers in buttoned-up khaki greatcoats, gaiters and all, arriving on French soil.

Some other things that happened, and troubled the Royal Family then, are almost forgotten. A sudden arrival *from* France, for instance: the King's predecessor, the Duke of Windsor, rushed over to seek some wartime responsibility. It was a request not easy to meet, for, in 1937, in exile, he had been an embarrassment if not a danger, visiting Hitler and his accomplices, expressing sympathy with the Nazis, and ingenuously signing autograph-books as 'Herzog Edward von Windsor'. However, he was asked to serve in the short-lived Military Mission in Paris. (After France fell, the Windsors remained for a while in the enemy-dominated Continent, drifting to 'neutral' Madrid and then Lisbon – a prey, it was reported, to agents from Berlin with Restoration plots on offer for the day when, as hoped, Germany would successfully invade Britain. Finally, the ex-king accepted from his brother a minor post, Governor of the distant Bahama Islands, and after the war he settled in France.)

But most indelible in the history of the war, from 1939 onwards, are the stories of how King George and Queen Elizabeth 'stayed put' in London as leaders of their people through five-and-a-half years of unprecedented peril and

Opposite At the height of the Blitz on London the King and Queen viewing the damage at the cinema attached to Madame Tussaud's.

suffering. Theirs, too, was the dreariness and the difficulty of day-to-day life, the shuttered windows and the sandbagged doors, the dark nights and dour days – all the grey austerity which was foreign to the nature of Queen Elizabeth in particular. True, the Palace sometimes had fresh eggs and vegetables from Windsor or from Sandringham, where their Norfolk country house was closed and the golf course ploughed up for food-growing. But for the most part they kept to the rules like ordinary people did. They knew about Spam and meatless rissoles, sugarless cakes and dried eggs, all the routines of the citizen's ration book. With the Queen giving instructions to the kitchens, 'managing on the coupons' became an art form; and her jokes with her daughters made 'Switch Off that Light' a delightful game as well as a duty order.

The two Princesses were sent off to live and do the schoolroom lessons at Windsor Castle where there was a strong deep shelter to sleep in when the air attacks came; and sometimes the parents went out to Windsor for the night. But Buckingham Palace was the home of the King and Queen, and the great house was grim and austere enough. In the middle of the war Mrs. Eleanor Roosevelt experienced a brief stay there, and was astonished at the cold and damp which had been allowed to creep in ('and just one little bar of an old electric fire in the room'), at the few inches of bath water, and at the canteen food which was served on the royal plates.

In 1940 – the year when the German armies swept across the Continent and the British Expeditionary Forces were humiliatingly (but miraculously by the bravery of hundreds of little ships) evacuated from the Dunkirk beaches – London became a rallying point for men and women who had emerged from the onslaught to continue in exile to fight for freedom. Buckingham Palace was for a time almost a refugee camp, for it gave hospitality to Heads of State from overrun countries who, evading Nazi drives to capture them as hostages, arrived in Britain as escapees.

One of those monarchs was the ageing Queen Wilhelmina of the Netherlands who, when she arrived and was received by the King and Queen, had a wardrobe consisting of only a tin hat and the torn clothes she stood up in. A British destroyer had rescued her. All she said was that she wanted taking back to her own country. She had to be told that the whole of Holland had fallen.

Another arrival was Norway's tall King Haakon. Like other guests-of-war at the Palace at this time, he was concerned at the British Royal Family's disregard of danger and the apparent lack of security around them. This worried the visitors because of their own first-hand experiences of being hunted by German troops, and because they had knowledge that there existed, now that Britain itself was under threat of invasion, an enemy plan to snatch the King and Queen and hold them hostage for the subservience of their subjects to Nazi conquerors.

Only when pressure had been put on Their Majesties to make them realize that their personal safety was a matter of importance was a two-room concrete and gas-proof shelter constructed below ground at the Palace. The idea of a bullet-proof car, even then, made Queen Elizabeth laugh and wrinkle her nose. She never at any time, even during the Blitzes, would accept travel along the roads in an armoured vehicle.

Doing an inelegant bolt downstairs from her own rooms when air-raid sirens sounded urgent alarm was not her habit. When ladies-in-waiting and servants were prudently descending to shelter, she was more likely to be discovered in unhurried progress through upstairs apartments gathering pet dogs and reading matter.

When things looked black for beleagured Britain, it was suggested that, whatever His Majesty did, the Queen and the two girls at any rate should leave the country for the safety of Canada. Her reply is legendary: 'The Princesses cannot go without me. I cannot go without the King. The King will never go.' And she took revolver-shooting practice.

Above The King and Queen inspect the damage caused by a delayed-action bomb at Buckingham Palace, which was hit altogether nine times in the war, mostly during the heavy bombing of 1940–41.

Opposite, top The christening in 1942 of Prince Michael, younger son of the Duke and Duchess of Kent, was attended by a large group of European royalty. (FRONT ROW, LEFT TO RIGHT) *Princess Elizabeth, Lady Patricia Ramsay, Queen Elizabeth, Prince Edward of Kent, Queen Mary, Princess Alexandra, the Duchess of Kent with the infant Prince Michael, the Dowager Marchioness of Milford Haven, Crown Princess Marthe of Norway, Princess Margaret and Princess Helena Victoria.* (BACK ROW) *Princess Marie Louise, Prince Bernhard of the Netherlands, King George VI, the Duke of Kent, King Haakon of Norway, King George of the Hellenes and Crown Prince Olav of Norway.*

Right Princess Elizabeth with her parents on her eighteenth birthday. The date was April 21, 1944.

Top *A smile from the Queen for the residents of Kennington, during a visit to the Duchy of Cornwall Estate in London in the early months of the war.*

Bottom *The Queen and Queen Mary were no less enthusiastic than the King in visiting troops and attended some of his inspections. Here they are seen with General Sir Oliver Leese on a visit to the Guards Second Division at Warminster in 1942.*

Her husband had declared that if invasion came he would join the resistance forces. The Blitzkrieg bombs rained down devastatingly, and it seemed as though the Luftwaffe attacks were a preliminary to assault by enemy troops as well as by enemy explosives. That was Battle of Britain year, 1940: Britain's darkest, and its finest hour. Secretly, in a mews at Windsor, a small motorized unit of Guardsmen were ready (if she had allowed it!) to take their Queen westward at the signal that the Germans had landed. But the signal did not come. Hitler's hordes – like Bonaparte's – never got across the Channel.

Against the odds, fighter squadrons of the Royal Air Force threw back Goering's sky armadas, and the only invasion barges left were shattered ones in the harbours of Occupied France. There were no landings, no paratroops in the Mall.

It is not beyond imagining that, if the foe *had* descended upon Winchelsea or Westminster they would have faced, in the echelons of opposition, a Boadicea in powder blue battling her way down to the front lines: Elizabeth.

Even as things were, you could not define *rear*-lines. Buckingham Palace itself was hit by bombs, flying bombs and rockets nine times, and the occupants had narrow escapes – experiences disclosed, and not by them, only after the war. One morning in 1940 the King and Queen were working on some papers with a Household official in a room overlooking the quadrangle when without warning the roar of an approaching aircraft was heard and a single German plane came screaming out of low cloud, straight down the line of the Mall's treetops. All in seconds, they saw a whole stick of bombs falling, right across the Palace. The King pulled his wife to the floor, where they lay with debris falling around them. As they got to their feet and into a corridor they heard, through the shattered windows, the sound of rushing water: columns of spray were shooting up in the quadrangle from burst mains and fractured sewers. Deep and noisome craters were spread across the grounds. Her Majesty had vivid recollections of the rat hunts which took place during the ensuing days.

In all the Palace bombings, casualties were light but much damage was done. Baths and buckets stood in state rooms and grand corridors to catch the rainwater which fell through roof holes. The Palace chapel was completely destroyed by a direct hit (on its site today stands the Queen's Gallery, where some of the royal art treasures are publicly exhibited).

The Queen was concerned to save, not so much her own furniture as national treasures in the London house and at Windsor, so as many objects as possible were taken away to safety. 'We were never sure what was going to disappear in the next raid,' she confessed later. 'We got Cecil Beaton to take photographs of pictures and of damage, as a matter of historical record. And because we thought that even Windsor might be partially destroyed, John Piper was asked to do a series of drawings of the Castle, 'to preserve its appearance for posterity'. (These Piper pictures, full of the feeling of Royal Windsor's stormy history, are today in the Lancaster Room of Clarence House, the Queen Mother's London home, where she recently said: 'Nothing terrible happened to Windsor. We now have both the Pipers and the Castle.')

After the first damaging of the Palace, Queen Elizabeth stood amid the wreckage and uttered the phrase which soon became famous: 'I'm almost glad we've been hit. I can now look the East End in the face.'

At the time of the intense air raids of 1940 and the sometimes even greater sufferings caused by the 'doodlebugs' and rockets later in the war, the King and Queen were often the first people from outside the neighbourhood to go to an area of devastation. Picking their way through the smoking rubble of buildings and the fountains of water from punctured fire hoses, whilst the living and the dead were being brought from collapsed houses, they would give what comfort they could to stricken people, knowing that even their presence was *some* support. Warnings of unexploded land-mines did not deter them. Such was the spirit of 'London can take it' that men and women would stand beside

Above *By August 1941 Sandringham Park had been ploughed up and planted out for war-time food production. Whenever they could, the Royal Family personally inspected their growing crops.*

Below *Mr Churchill with the King and Queen on the steps of Number 10 Downing Street, October 1941.*

the ambulances and the wreckage of their homes, waving, giving the thumbs-up sign, and offering mugs of black-brewed tea to the gaunt figure in uniform and the resolute wife beside him.

Not only were the blitzed areas of the capital visited. The Queen, sometimes without the King, went to hospitals, air-raid shelters, fire stations and first-aid posts in many parts of the country. Together they travelled half a million miles in the Royal train, sleeping on board when the carriages were shunted overnight into sidings where railway Home Guards stood watch against any possible attention from saboteurs or 'fifth column' fanatics. Frequently the two people from the Palace were at ack-ack gun sites, barrage-balloon posts, airfields, munition factories, army camps. Liverpool, Hull, Portsmouth, Bath, Swansea, Coventry, and other sites of bombed-ruins and

Below *In June 1943 King George VI had been in Tripoli meeting some of the heroes of the Desert War. He chatted with patients at a hospital for British troops under the eye of their commander, General Montgomery.*

Opposite, top *When they were young . . . the King and Queen with Princesses Elizabeth and Margaret during a week-end at Windsor.*

Above *In July 1937 Queen Elizabeth, as Colonel-in-Chief, visited the armoured section of the Queen's Bays at Aldershot.*

Opposite, bottom *Whenever duties allowed, the Royal Family would gather round the piano at Royal Lodge, Windsor.*

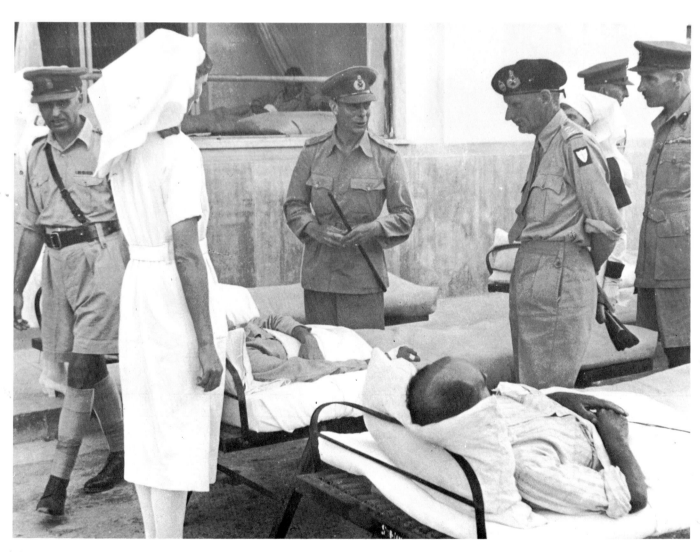

barrack-rooms saw the couple arrive quietly and move along, talking with every kind of war worker. Elizabeth's talent for listening was employed as naturally as ever. Her sympathetic questioning was the point of hundreds of stories. When the Americans had come over, before D-Day, a homesick sergeant at a United States army base told his buddies, in homespun tribute: 'Gosh, that was a swell lady. Talked to me like she was Mom. And was sure interested in every darn thing, even my old man's stomach ulcer.'

Trails of brightness were left behind wherever the Queen had stepped. Her own anxieties and sorrows were not paraded, though the Royal Family suffered personal losses like everybody else. King George's brother, the Duke of Kent, who after a naval career had become an Air Force officer, was killed in a flying accident on active service in the summer of 1942.

Princess Elizabeth and Princess Margaret spent the Hitler years out of the limelight and in the sombreness of Windsor Castle; but their mother saw to it that they were not only educated but from time to time had their lives brightened by a birthday party or an informal dance. Men who in that period were young Guards officers based at army depots nearby remember being invited over to the Castle by the Queen to what were real 'knees-up' evenings with games and music after supper, and highly informal dances punctuated by a ringing royal voice calling 'Away you go, Lieutenant, dance with Elizabeth and don't be shy!' It became a routine that the Queen and the King led the congas round the ballroom.

The annual Christmas pantomimes put on at the Castle were highlights. The Princesses starred in these; and uniformed servicemen augmented royal staffs to form packed audiences, greatly enjoying themselves. One time the elder daughter would be Prince Charming and the younger one Cinderella. Notably, there was the '43 staging of *Aladdin*, in which, it was said, Princess Elizabeth was at her most animated. Perhaps it was because a young Lieutenant Philip Mountbatten was with her parents, watching from the front row of the 'stalls' in the echoing Waterloo Chamber.

In 1942, when she was sixteen, Princess Elizabeth lost no time in registering for National Service like any other young woman. She put on her Girl Guide clothes to visit the Labour Exchange and do it. Two years later, having persuaded her parents to let her join a uniformed corps and at least serve on the Home Front, she entered the Auxiliary Territorial Service and in due course became a Junior Officer in a Mechanical Transport Training Centre at Aldershot. Her official registration read: 'No. 230873, Second Subaltern Elizabeth Alexandra Mary Windsor. Age: 18. Eyes: Blue. Hair: Brown. Height: 5ft 3ins.'

Her daughter's A.T.S. enthusiasm at the time was reflected in the Queen's crack that 'we had sparking plugs all last night at dinner'.

Various members of the Royal Family had been mobilized earlier: the stolid Uncle Harry, Duke of Gloucester, served with the Army, and his sister Princess Mary was in A.T.S. khaki throughout the war. Of the two Windsor Princesses' generation, only Viscount Lascelles (Princess Mary's son, now the Earl of Harewood) was old enough to go into battle: a young Grenadier, he was wounded and captured on the Italian front. The girls' other cousins were either very young or not yet in existence when the war started. Prince Eddie, today's Duke of Kent, was almost four and his sister, Princess Alexandra, two-and-a-half. Prince Michael was an infant only one month old in 1942 when their

Right *Their Majesties, wearing their gasmask haversacks, leave St. Paul's Cathedral on the Day of National Prayer in October 1939. The Lord Mayor of London is behind the king.*

Below *The King and Queen stop to chat with schoolchildren during their Victory Tour of South London a few days after the German surrender.*

King George VI takes the salute as the mechanised column passes during the Victory Procession on June 8, 1946.

ather was killed. William of Gloucester and his brother Richard today's Duke) were both wartime babies. Unlike Elizabeth and Margaret, they do not remember the hostilities or the war's nding.

It was in May of 1945 that peace at last was proclaimed with he surrender of Germany. And on the Victory-in-Europe Day, Buckingham Palace was the magnet for huge crowds. They tood, a surging mass of cheering and singing people, outside the ailings until well after midnight, time after time demanding ppearances on the Palace balcony from the King and Queen, he two Princesses, and Prime Minister Churchill.

Japan had still to be defeated – that came at the end of August - but there was great thankfulness that the main menace, Hitler's Germany, had been overcome by the Allies.

The King and Queen had special thought for their daughters n that V.E.-Night of wild public jubilation. 'Poor darlings', said heir father, 'they've never had any fun yet'. So, with the Queen's agreement, the two of them, after several balcony ppearances, and then at the Princesses' request, slipped out of a de-entrance to the Palace. Not alone, it is true. The Queen ommandeered a little party of young Guards officers to take are of the Princesses. The group then plunged into the dense hrongs of dancing and shouting celebrators (under the orgotten luxury of street lights) and were borne en masse, often arried off their feet, along the Mall and down Whitehall. Princess Elizabeth, then 19, was in her A.T.S. uniform and she ulled her khaki cap well down over her eyes because she was errified of being recognized, but was told by an officer that she nust 'wear uniform properly', as she recalled to the present vriter in a commemorative B.B.C. interview exactly forty years ater as she (the Queen then, of course) looked back to that nique experience.

In fact, neither Princess Elizabeth nor Princess Margaret were

ever spotted, though they were out in the streets for two hours – the first and only time in her life that the present Queen has mingled with her people completely incognito.

Her Majesty's words in that 1985 recollection of 1945 were: 'I think we went on the balcony nearly every hour, six times, and then when the excitements of the floodlights being switched on got through to us, my sister and I realized that *we* couldn't see what the crowds were enjoying as they looked up at the balcony. My mother had put her tiara on for the occasion, so we asked my parents if we could go out and see for ourselves. Down in the crowds, we cheered the King and Queen and then walked miles through the streets. Coming back, we stood outside the Palace and shouted "We want the King!" and were successful in seeing my parents on the balcony yet again at midnight, having cheated slightly because we sent a message into the house to say we were waiting outside. I think it was one of the most memorable moments of my life.'

It was indeed a heady time; and in the weeks that followed, people luxuriated in the sheer relief of peaceful nights, no blackout curtains at the windows, no wondering whether the sound of an aircraft engine was 'one of theirs'. Peace, but still privation: rationing was to go on for several years. Those weeks and months after the war in Europe gave everybody time to reflect glumly on all the shortages which had perforce been 'put up with' during life-or-death hostilities but now, alas, seemed to have come to stay.

And there were the residual family anxieties. At the Palace, the Queen worried over her husband's obvious tiredness. The past five years, as she could see more plainly now, had taken their toll of a man far from shockproof.

It was a measure of George the Sixth's sensitiveness to the setbacks and misfortunes of others that he was grieved by what he felt was the 'ungrateful rejection' of his friend Churchill in the General Election of July 1945. The verdict of that election's polling meant that Winston, the Prime Minister who had become the Monarch's counsellor – and had put great value on the *King's* counsel too – Winston S. Churchill, the man who had led Britain to victory and the world out of jackboot thrall, was unambiguously dismissed by demobilized voters craving a Brave New World.

The world with which George VI was now concerned was the world of the ruling Labour Party and Mr. Attlee, the atomic bomb and President Truman. Politics were back to peacetime wrangle. As to domestic life, that was still depressingly restricted throughout Britain. Unrelieved control by ration-books, queues for food, successive economic crises which brought spending cuts – all those factors meant a hangover of drabness in the land. Austerity conditioned the existences of the King and Queen as well as their people, and the sheer dinginess of those post-war years was foreign to Queen Elizabeth's nature. She in particular longed for a return to brightness and colour. She had entered the war as a young married woman, had stood up cheerfully to the dangers of the times and also to the ugliness of them, the hardness of years in which it was a virtue to accept plain discomfort uncomplainingly; and now, as Queen Consort in her mid-forties, she was required to respect the deadly pace at which gracious things began to return to a weary world.

Below *A view of the Waterloo Chamber in Windsor Castle in its normal splendour. For fear of damage from German bombs, the grand paintings hung on the walls were removed to safety, but, at the instigation of the King and Queen, the dismally-emptied picture frames were filled with cheerful pantomime drawings of such characters as Aladdin and Red Riding Hood, shown in the photograph above.*

Left *View of the Sunken Garden from the East Front Rooms of the Castle.*

Below *View of the East Front of the Castle. It is from these windows, in the private apartments, that the Queen views the Garden.*

CHAPTER SEVEN

PEACE – AND TRAGEDY

THE ENDING of World War Two hostilities did not, alas, bestow any real peace among nations, but, rather, it brought the fearful age of the Nuclear Bomb. But at any rate, the shooting and the explosions had stopped, and one could indulge in hope. By the end of 1945 the King and Queen had been able quietly to demobilize themselves and ease back into regular peacetime occasions. Pleasant routines of State and relaxed public appearances were resumed; and that was something refreshing to the Queen, who, besides having become a complete professional in her job, knew that the King with her help had come to full stature and assurance in his duties. Though frail, he was equal to tackling normal kingship.

And the Family were able to be together again. What was more – as her mother was quick to discern – romance had blossomed for the Heir to the Throne. Princess Elizabeth was in love with her cousin Philip, and there was no denying that the good-looking extrovert Lieutenant Mountbatten, R.N. was in the same state towards her. The high-speed arrivals of his sports car at a side entrance to palace or castle were habitual week-end phenomena.

An engagement might have been announced at Christmas 1946 (the Princess was only 20 then, and Philip 25), but Her Royal Highness's parents wished there to be at least a pause. For one thing, in the New Year of 1947 Their Majesties were committed to a long tour, nearly four months altogether, through what was then the Dominion of South Africa, taking both the Princesses with them. So no announcement until after that.

Not that they disapproved of the young Mountbatten. But they felt that the break, the absence of the Princess in a far country, would give the eager couple a situation full of other interests which would force them fully to know their own minds and be quite sure of their wishes. Away they went, then, King and Queen and daughters, away from what was probably the most arctic British winter of modern times (the conscientious King at one moment considered quite seriously a return from the African sunshine to share the shivers and the burst pipes being

Opposite Princess Elizabeth and Lieutenant Philip Mountbatten *photographed after the announcement of their betrothal in July 1947.*

endured by his subjects at home), away by sea in H.M.S. *Vanguard*, latest and last battleship of the Royal Navy.

Once on land, the journeys were made in unprecedented fashion. For two full months and for ten thousand miles they travelled – and lived – on rails in the White Train, whose fourteen coaches made a motorized caravan almost half a mile long. A Court and a Government on wheels. Each day the principals would leave the train and make far forays by road, meeting every kind of inhabitant of the vast Union and adjacent territories at official engagements and very many informal gatherings. That train was home, its couches and its communications alike excellent. The King could speak by telephone to any part of the world – the Princess could, and did, get calls to her Philip in England.

Queen Elizabeth was a centre of attraction throughout South Africa – everything they expected of a Queen; and more, sometimes unpredictably more. There was a day, for instance, when equerries and ladies-in-waiting held their breath in momentary horror. An old Afrikaner who had fought in the Boer Wars entered a line of local officials being presented to the visitors and when, bearing a grudge and bent on offensiveness, he stood in front of Her Majesty, he growled: 'I can never forgive the English for what they did to my country.' Gasps all round – but not from the Queen. The Bowes-Lyon blue eyes flashed brightly as with a smile she replied: 'Oh I do so understand. We in Scotland often feel very much the same.' The wind was taken clean out of the man's sails; and he formed a new opinion about British royalty.

But it was Princess Elizabeth who was the star of the show three days before the tour's end. She became 21 years old on April 21, and the best-remembered celebration of that birthday was her broadcast, from the garden of Government House in Capetown, to the peoples of the Commonwealth, pledging that 'My whole life, whether it be long or short, shall be devoted to your service'.

She was of course in fine spirits, for it was the voyage home now. She had relished the tour, even if not the separation from Philip. About him, she was 'quite sure'. And within two months of the family's arrival back in Britain her betrothal to Philip – now of British nationality – was made public. It was a popular announcement.

The wedding, its details brightly supervised by the bride's mother, took place on November 20, 1947. The Order of Service papers in Westminster Abbey said that the Princess was marrying 'Lieutenant Philip Mountbatten', although the King had conferred the title of Duke of Edinburgh on the man who was taking away his Lilibet. The creation of Philip as a royal Duke had been an act which the King had kept secret until the night before the marriage, and there was no time to alter the printing on the papers already in place on the Abbey seats.

In London the wedding was a gala day. You had to be out and about to see it all, for although the service was fully broadcast on the radio, television's cameras inside the church still had only a foothold: some restricted filming by them was permitted. Pavements and windows all along the processional routes to and from the church were packed with people. Britain had not yet emerged from the post-war drabness, but the authorities had allowed, just for the day, some decorations and many splashes of the old pre-war pageantry (and, despite full-force rationing, the bride had extra clothing coupons for the making of her dress). The processional cavalcades were a brief but heart-warming gleam in a 'utility' world still dull and difficult, its men scarcely out of khaki. We had not seen the Household troopers in their full-dress splendour for almost a decade.

Those royal processions, this time to and from St. Paul's Cathedral, were again acclaimed less than six months later when, on April 26, 1948, King George VI and Queen Elizabeth celebrated their Silver Wedding by attending a service of thanksgiving for twenty-five years of married happiness. Characteristically, in a broadcast that night, the Queen spoke not only of her loved home and family, but also of many others in her thoughts, who could not at that time have such felicity. 'My heart goes out,' she said, 'to all who are living in uncongenial surroundings and who are longing for the time when they will have a home of their own'. The words were appreciated by many listeners who were in temporary lodgings or living with relatives in the crowded houses of patched-up streets still gap-toothed from Hitler's bombs.

Above *Queen Elizabeth chats with Winston Churchill after the marriage of the then Marquess of Blandford and Miss Susan Hornby.*

Below *Quiet thanksgiving after the drive through cheering crowds. In 1948 King George VI and Queen Elizabeth had been married twenty-five years. The Silver Wedding service was held in St. Paul's Cathedral on April 26.*

Opposite *Elizabeth-and-Philip wedding day, 1947 – the official picture.*

Another date in history, and of great public interest, was November 14 in the same year, 1948, when Princess Elizabeth gave birth to her first child, Charles Philip Arthur George, today's Prince of Wales, first of a new generation. The Queen was 'Grannie' for the first time, proud and glad about the 'Charles', a name that glows in the Scottish history to which she has always been romantically and knowledgeably attached. Crowds assembled and cheered and sang in front of Buckingham Palace when the news was known; and, at the other end of the Mall, the fountains in Trafalgar Square became coloured – 'blue for a boy'.

But it was shadow as well as sunshine for the Palace that year. Concern over the King's health began to worry his family. The seriousness of his physical state was not at first known to the public, and indeed not fully to the Princess in the months of her pregnancy, for her father had insisted that the extent of his suffering should be kept from her until after the birth of the baby.

The fact was that, as a new life entered the family, the tide of the grandfather's life began to ebb: when Prince Charles was born, George VI was lying ill under the same roof. Abdication and Armageddon had taken their toll, but the trouble was more than a legacy of the strain of the years. When specialists were called to investigate the cramp in the legs of which His Majesty was complaining, hardening of the arteries and danger of gangrene were found. A public announcement, cancellation of engagements, a period of complete rest indoors – all these had to follow – and once more a heavy burden of anxiety and extra work lay upon the Queen. Though distressed at this misfortune to a husband who was only beginning his middle years, she maintained an outward calm and self-control which has been a mainstay of her make-up throughout her life. She fulfilled many of what would have been the Sovereign's outside engagements, at the same time keeping the King restfully and agreeably occupied whilst medical treatment kept him indoors. Her presence was a blessing to patient and doctors alike.

The King responded well to his treatment and was fit enough to go to Sandringham and make his Christmas broadcast. Early in 1949 he was able personally to hold an investiture at the Palace, though he bestowed the accolades and insignia sitting down.

But the King's right leg was still obstructed, and an operation, a lumbar sympathectomy, was successfully performed in March. From that time onwards, however, the King was compelled permanently to moderate his manner of life, abandoning all but the gentler duties. The Queen took on two people's work with resolution and optimism. She was a pillar of both domestic duty and public life. Nor was there a carefree existence for Princess Elizabeth in those early years of married life. She had to trim much of her time of what should have been private enjoyment as wife of a naval officer serving at agreeable home and overseas stations, and, even at that stage, she began to take on some of the royal duties that should have been her father's. Her growing family were her own joy, and his too. Princess Elizabeth's second child, Anne, was born on August 15, 1950 – at Clarence House, which Princess Elizabeth and the Duke of Edinburgh had at that time made their home.

In the Spring of 1951 the King managed to play his part at the formal opening of the Festival of Britain, with its exciting and eccentric buildings on the South Bank of the Thames; but soon afterwards he suffered catarrhal inflammation of a lung. A malignant growth was discovered: the lung had to be removed.

The King and Queen, with Princess Margaret, driving through the crowded streets after their Silver Wedding thanksgiving service in St. Paul's.

The operation of 'lung resection' was carried out in a Palace room which had been turned into an operating theatre. Concern for the Monarch's life rose to a high pitch, but he slowly and bravely came through the ordeal, depressed though he was, not only about his own condition but his country's economic crisis and the war in Korea.

Doctors and nurses in the Palace at the time spoke with admiration and amazement of the conduct of the Queen, the quiet stamina and style she radiated, hardly leaving her husband's bedside for a week, bringing a loving and confident influence to bear not only on the patient but on the entire team who were ministering around him.

In the late autumn of 1951 Queen Elizabeth, with the King,

should have been away on a big tour in North America, for which Canada in particular had been preparing for twelve months. But such things were out of the question, even though His Majesty was alive and apparently making a good recovery. So, as representatives of Sovereign and Consort, Princess Elizabeth and the Duke of Edinburgh (already objects of much interest overseas) were dutifully dispatched to spend October and November travelling across Canada from Atlantic to Pacific and back: a major tour that had major welcomes everywhere, not least in Washington, U.S.A. for two days, with President Harry Truman as an avuncular host.

The Princess, anxious about her father and on the telephone to London almost daily, knew she might not see the King again –

and knew also that in the official baggage on the royal train was a sealed envelope containing a draft Declaration of Accession (her own accession to the Throne) in case the worst happened.

Happily, the King was well convalescent and gently working when the travellers returned late in the year. He had gained strength and, though not easily, made another Christmas Day broadcast, this time a short message and not delivered 'live'. His operation had accentuated his breathing and speech difficulties. So, during the December of 1951 B.B.C. technicians went to the Palace and painstakingly recorded the Royal Message phrase by phrase, until the fragments on the tapes could finally be joined to make a complete statement. On that Christmas afternoon, George the Sixth, free from the tension he had always felt when

facing the microphone, could relax in the calm of his room up there in Norfolk and listen to himself on the radio. It had been a singularly brave effort, that husky speech; and it was his last one. The sound of his words and message of simple faith – the counting of his blessings – brought tears to the eyes of listeners and apprehension to millions of hearts.

And yet, early in 1952, he himself declared that he felt, comparatively, so much better in body and in spirit that he could send Princess Elizabeth and Prince Philip, in his stead, on what was to have been a five months' tour of Australia and New Zealand, visiting Kenya on the way. On a bitterly cold last day of January 1952 he went, with the Queen and Princess Margaret, to see his daughter and son-in-law leave London by air.

No one who was present at London Airport that day can forget what was to prove the last sight of George VI. Inside the lounge at Heathrow the *au revoirs* were said; there were more family goodbyes inside the waiting aircraft; then down the steps and out came King and Queen and Margaret; and we saw a last wave from Elizabeth and Philip before the plane's door closed on them and the Argonaut taxied slowly away into the distant wintry haze at the beginning of the runway. The King stood on the starkly exposed tarmac, bareheaded, his face gaunt and strained, his hair in windswept disorder, straining his eyes to watch the aircraft climb into the leaden sky. Only after the last speck of it was lost to view was he persuaded by the Queen to go inside to the warmth of the airport building.

It was the last farewell to his Lilibet. And it was as though he knew it. One week later he was dead, and his daughter back on that same spot at the airport – not Princess Elizabeth, but reigning Queen.

Yet when death struck, it caught those about him unawares. Straight from that airfield, George the Sixth and his wife and

Above *A carefree afternoon on the moors in 1949.*

Opposite, top *This was when King George VI (in 1951, the year befo his death) was broadcasting to the world that the great Festival of Brita was open. The speech was made from the portico of St. Paul's, after a service of Festival dedication.*

their younger daughter had gone at once to his beloved Sandringham House, his birthplace. Awaiting him were a few friends – and a few days. There he seemed content, relaxed now, glad to be resting in the peace of the Norfolk countryside. On February 5, which was the traditional Keepers' Day and had crisp bright weather, he spent much of the daylight hours on the estate, enjoying some rough shooting with the specially-lightweight gun he had begun to use. He planned the next day's sport, spent a happy evening in the house, with Princess Margaret playing the piano as he liked her to do, and retired to his room at 10.30. One of the staff, out in the garden, saw him fixing the catch of his window at about midnight. During that night he died peacefully in his sleep.

And so there passed away – at what hour nobody can know, for he was dead when his valet went to wake him next morning – a devoted and diligent monarch who worked unceasingly at the tasks thrust upon him, with unstinted effort and to good effect. Now he would struggle no more, this high-strung and wholly honest man who might have seemed in 1936 a sad Surrogate Sovereign but who had grown to be one of our best and best-loved kings. He lived only fifty-six years, and now his Queen was a widow at fifty-one.

Their elder daughter, Elizabeth, at once no longer Heir Apparent but Sovereign Queen at the age of twenty-five, flew home from Africa in the black clothes of mourning which,

86

The new King and Queen follow the Coronation year Grand National through their glasses.

significantly, had been in her travelling wardrobes. Four thousand miles away in Kenya, her world tour scarcely begun, the great change in her life had come upon her in the strangest of circumstances. She and the Duke of Edinburgh had been in East Africa when the news of her father's death reached her on February 6, 1952. That death, the 'Demise of the Crown', had automatically made her Queen during the night just ended, though she did not then know it. She and the Duke had, strangely, spent the night watching big game from the lofty verandah of a tree-house above a water hole deep in the Aberdare Forests, almost on the Equator. The fateful news from England arrived next morning. She had become Queen whilst up a tree.

Although for two years Princess Elizabeth had known that the King's death might come at any time, the shock of losing this loved parent was grievous.

But the blow fell heaviest upon her mother Queen Elizabeth, 'that most valiant woman', as Winston Churchill described her in his sonorous tribute at that time. Her life, her position, was utterly changed. Bertie was gone. She had been at his side with faith and devotion in days of joy and sorrow, war and peace, for almost three decades; and although she bore the premature ending of a cherished partner's life with every sign of control and courage, the grief was very painful, and very private; and even more exemplary in the face of what was the loss, for her, of a

Opposite *The infant Prince Charles, who slept peacefully throughout his christening on December 15, 1948, is held by Queen Elizabeth in the Music Room of Buckingham Palace.*

Above *Prince Charles gets his share of attention after the christening of Princess Anne on October 2, 1950.*

whole pattern of existence. At a stroke, the posts and prerogatives of Queen Consort were hers no more and she was thrust into a loneliness which not even a family's love could assuage. She was not mistress of a palace, not the Power Beside the Throne. Her first daughter was First Lady now, walking the path of service for which her mother with tolerant wisdom had trained her.

At once, unhesitatingly and not for a moment overshadowing, the mother gave to the new young Queen her loyalty and unique support. The reign of Queen Elizabeth the Second had begun.

Above *January 1952. The Royal Family leaving Drury Lane Theatre on the eve of the departure of Princess Elizabeth and the Duke of Edinburgh for what should have been a tour of Kenya, Ceylon, Australia and New Zealand. In fact they had reached only Kenya when the King died a week later.*

Left *Three Queens – Queen Elizabeth II, Queen Mary and Queen Elizabeth The Queen Mother – in mourning for King George VI.*

Opposite *With Prince Charles and Princess Anne on the terrace of Royal Lodge in April 1954. A prized picture from the family album.*

CHAPTER EIGHT

SWEET RETURN

WHAT NEXT, then, for the mother who was now only *Parent Queen*, and yet had become a loved figure on the world stage? Many of us wondered what would happen. The rocking-chair of retirement? At any rate she was not to be called 'Queen *Dowager*'. Couldn't be, for that dim title in our history creaks of age and unimportance. ('Queen Dynamo', colloquially, would always have been more fitting.) So when the style of 'Queen Mother' was uniquely made the official one, it was absolutely right.

But what part was she to play? Were we going to lose her? It might be so. How could anybody dream, then, in 1952, that 'the best was yet to be', and that she would carry the monarchy forward through the *second* half of the century!

The impression that she *was* going to disappear and put herself as far away from London as possible was strengthened when it was learned that Her Majesty, having vanished grief-stricken to Scotland, had suddenly purchased for herself a distant and doubtful little sixteenth-century castle on the bleak northern-most coast of the Scottish mainland, a dilapidated old place that looked ripe for demolition, riddled as it was with the damp and the black peat smoke of centuries: the Castle of Mey. That old pile of pink stone was an unprepossessing house which not many people knew, even people in that north-eastern part of windswept Caithness. It stands gaunt above a beach and flat farmland a dozen miles east of Thurso, and seems prey to all the storms of the Pentland Firth. It was then called – by those who could recall any name at all – Barrogill Castle. It was for sale, with no purchaser in prospect.

Queen Elizabeth saw the place in the early days after the King's death, when she had gone to stay with old friends in Caithness and was driving one afternoon along the coast road that goes to John O'Groats. She went down to have a look, and was seized by an impulse. Something about the house and its setting and history appealed to the Scot in her. Inquiries were made, and when she learned that the likely fate of the castle was a pulling-down or abandonment to final crumbling she became

Opposite Delight all round as Grannie holds five-month-old Prince Andrew in the garden of Clarence House. It was Her Majesty's sixtieth birthday.

sure. 'Never!' she said. 'It mustn't be lost. It is part of Scotland's heritage. *I'll* buy it.'

Which she promptly did, and gave back to it the name, Mey, which it had when the Sinclairs built it four hundred years ago, before it passed in later generations into the possession of the Earls of Caithness. She at once set about restoring the castle's appearance, beginning gradually the installing of equipment that would make it habitable, and then furnishing rooms to her own taste. It all took several years and a lot of money; and the royal owner kept up intense personal interest in the whole transformation. She was *au fait* with every detail: even the plumbers' operations and the buying of cooking stoves.

Today, Mey has long become the lady's loved haven in the Far North. Not for many weeks each year is she in residence, but she is never out of touch. She knows about the sheep on the adjoining croft which she owns, about the health of her Aberdeen Angus herd, about the marketing of the produce from the gardens. Even when in London she is as avid a reader of *The John O'Groat Journal* as of *The Times*.

During the short spring and summer sojourns at Mey, Her Majesty enjoys every day, whatever the weather – members of little house parties up there have told of her impish delight in hauling them, and her dogs, out into the horizontal rain on some picnic excursion and squatting down to eat sandwiches in a dripping barn. What she has liked is that she has been able to go about among the Caithness folk without being harassed by inquisitive crowds. She can walk up the street in Thurso on shopping expeditions and chat with all and sundry, a fellow country-woman. Mey is her own, a far little kingdom to possess, private and personal, the antithesis of pomp.

So, buying that castle in 1952 *did* give the answer to the question whether the widowed Queen was going to fade into inactivity and become unknown: the answer was decidedly in the negative. Mey was a blessing, not a bolt-hole. She disappeared to the North for a while in the early weeks of that year. She wished to be quiet, of course she did. But it was a break before back to work. This Queen Elizabeth had too strong a pull on the affections of the British people to be allowed to go. Nor did she intend to abandon duty. Soon after the King's death she had quietly declared: 'My only wish is that I may be allowed to continue to do the work that we sought to do together.' Nothing more perfectly puts the situation than two lines John Milton wrote:

> For solitude sometimes is best society,
> And short retirement urges sweet return.

The return, as indelible history knows, was to her life's longest phase, to a 'third life' of joyful work in the public gaze, to decades of service, and to new chapters of astonishing activity in a great variety of fields. A full life as the legendary, perennial 'Queen Mum'.

But the first step out of loneliness and back into the warmth of world regard was probably not easy. Much more difficult it would have been, however, had the occasion not been in Scotland. Three months after the King's death, she flew from Windsor up to Fife to bid farewell and godspeed to 'her own' soldiers, the Black Watch, Royal Highlanders, the family regiment, whose treasured Colonel-in-Chief she had been ever since '37, the year in which their 'lassie from Glamis' had been crowned a Queen. For now the First Battalion had been ordered to the war in Korea. She *had* to see them. And there was no half-measure about the commitment.

She carried out an inspection and without hesitation addressed the parade of five hundred men, each officer wearing the dark armband of mourning. She talked with the soldiers' relatives and regimental Old Comrades; she saw the men's quarters, not neglecting to take a canty dram in the sergeants' mess. Later, she was entertained well in the officers' mess, and it was a late night.

Some weeks later came a much remembered surprise. The scene was a remote hillside above Balmoral, from which castle the Queen Mother had risen unexpectedly early to greet territorials of the regiment. Through the cold mist tramped a long line of khaki men, single file with rifles slung, looking a thought downcast in the inhospitable dawn. Then, suddenly, backs straightened and shoulders were squared beneath the capes; salutes snapped out with a quick eyes-right, and the pipes sounded. For there – 5 a.m. though it was – stood a redoubtable female figure, steadfast upon a heathery tussock beside a drystone wall. It was the Colonel-in-Chief herself, this time wrapped in a thick woolly overcoat and an old felt hat. She had a corgi beside her and a smile on her face.

She was back on duty, and in character.

Meanwhile, in '52, it was the new young Queen who was of course the prime target of publicity. There were pictures galore of Elizabeth II, news sheets and magazines going 'over the top' with euphoria about the 'dawn of a new Elizabethan age', headed by a fresh Buckingham Palace family, 'handsome husband and wife and two nice youngsters named Charles and Anne, bless them'.

Yet – despite all that furore, and no matter how much the widowed parent stood back whilst giving fullest support to the young monarch – attention and affection never ceased to be given to Queen Mother Elizabeth and her renewed pattern of busy public duties, enjoyed by her simply because 'life is for working, not idling'.

Sadly, the Queen Mother was in mourning again in March 1953 when Britain's royal scene lost that steely dowager, the straight-backed, toque-topped lady of the proprieties and parasols, predatory amasser of antique furniture and pictures – Queen Mary. She died, at the age of 87, at her London home, Marlborough House, a stone's throw from St. James's Palace. 'No postponing of my granddaughter's Coronation if I am gone

During a visit to Caithness in the early months of her widowhood, Queen Elizabeth was told there was a possibility that old Barrogill Castle would be demolished. She decided there and then to buy it for her own use. Once the castle was restored she gave it the ancient name of the Castle of Mey, and it is to this retreat that she goes whenever she can. Here an informal Mey basks in the warm August sunshine, when Her Majesty was in residence.

before then,' was her last wish. The death, in fact, came just two months before the Crowning.

Very shortly before that great event, the Queen Mother and her Queen-daughter changed homes. The new Monarch and her family were installed at Buckingham Palace, and the mother (Princess Margaret with her) moved down the Mall to take up her long residence in Clarence House, St. James's Palace.

A few words on that dwelling can properly be interjected here, because 'Clarence House' and 'Queen Mother' have become almost synonymous; and it was in 1953 that the natural connexion began. The House, solid and unpretentious with high garden wall making it not easy to see, takes its name from the time when the Duke of Clarence who was George III's third son lived there. Indeed he stayed on and lived there even when he became King William IV, the bluff and rather eccentric 'sailor king'. During the first forty years of *this* century the Duke of Connaught who was Queen Victoria's third son, succeeding an earlier Duke of Edinburgh who was his brother, was the royal inhabitant. In the Second World War, Clarence House was for a long time the headquarters of the Red Cross.

The place had to be much restored when it became the first home of the then Princess Elizabeth and the Duke of Edinburgh after they married in 1947, but only when Queen Elizabeth went there in widowhood in '53 did it become the warm and gracious home that many modern years have now known, a home in which the lady's elegant taste is proclaimed throughout its interior. There are of course classic pictures of horses; and inherited treasures from the past: Lely, Allan Ramsey and Hoppner are there. But specially familiar to all Her Majesty's staff and Household, uniformed or not, (and, who knows, by the corgis too, who are called 'my faithful friends'?) are the modern pictures represented by Sisley, Sickert, Wilson Steer, Paul Nash, Sidney Nolan and others. For she has collected them.

And pictures of Herself. She is *the* favourite of all the portrait painters who have had the chance of sittings. There is a big Augustus John of her, hanging in a place of prominence above the fireplace in the spacious Garden Room. It is an odd one, the face strange, and no wonder, for it is a portrait unfinished. The bombs of the 1940 Blitz interrupted the sittings, but when London was a little quieter Her Majesty sent a message to the artist saying she was willing for the work to be completed – 'if you at your studio have any windows, for we have none here in Buckingham Palace, and it is too dark and dusty anyway.' John never responded; and long after the war someone found the canvas lying deep in spiders' webs in a cellar. It was cleaned, framed, and given to the sitter. Now it is enshrined, an honoured curio.

But – to return to the story of the Queen Mother's life in historic 1953 – Clarence House came into full occupation then, but the surpassing centre of attraction in that year was about one mile to the south-east of the mansion: Westminster Abbey, where the crowning of the new Queen took place on June 2. Work had been going on there for many months before the great occasion, and when the day came the interior of the huge church had been transformed by galleries and rich decorations into what seemed like a magnificent theatre, with seating for seven thousand, over three times the number of a maximum congregation for an ordinary service there. And amid the glittering pageantry of her daughter's Coronation as Elizabeth II, the Royal Mother is

Dominions overseas had particularly strongly opposed such a marriage: that, no doubt, was the reason for the reference to the Commonwealth, the unique organization which has always meant a great deal to Queen Elizabeth, even in recent years of strain upon it.

The Townsend experience has long ago passed into history, but not out of memory. Peter himself has written that 'the Queen Mother was never anything but considerate in her attitude to me, to us both, throughout the whole difficult affair'.

Looking back, the episode may seem to today's minds very odd and old-fashioned and sadly wrong in its ending (the Princess could have fought on, and eventually have obtained the marriage through civil law). The events could quite probably have had a different turn had they happened nowadays, for the climate of morals has changed and we live in a permissive society. Yet the *royal* law – of prohibition and need of 'special permission' when a divorced person is concerned – is still unchanged. It still applies to possible marriages of all King George II's descendants in the royal line.

In 1960, less than five years after Peter Townsend's departure from the story, Princess Margaret married the talented professional photographer, Anthony Armstrong-Jones, who was later made Earl of Snowdon; and the partnership produced two happy children, David, Viscount Linley, and Lady Sarah Armstrong-Jones – a delightful young woman, favourite with all the family. But the marriage later ran into troubled waters, and in 1976 the Princess and her husband – two very volatile and artistic human beings – decided to separate; and the marriage was dissolved in '78. Lord Snowdon married again. Far from being ostracized, he is liked, he has continued to be welcomed in royal homes, and has taken many pictures of royal occasions and their people.

Any diary list of the royal occasions and appointments of any one of the peak Queen Mother Years makes almost unbelievable reading: few royal figures in history can have 'taken on' so much and 'taken it easy' so little. Enjoying it all, too. Her activities in the Fifties and Sixties astonished even her own experienced Household. An austere history-summary might log that, having become a widow, she had now no constitutional position whatever. True. But she did not need it. She was the one and only 'Queen Mum', everybody's charmer, and wanted by everybody. The number of public functions she performed at home and literally round the world exceeded, it seemed, those of the Monarch and half the Royal Family put together.

Stories of her versatility are legion. One facet of her life was her twenty-five years as Chancellor of the University of London, that great complex of student activity, which began in 1955. It was a time rich in reminiscences and permissible nostalgia. She explored every University college, school, club, post-graduate institute and hall of residence. The outdoor events too: those struck the chords of sporting life that were within her. In boathouses and pavilions men recall her sprightly encouragement to Varsity crews from the banks of a windblown Thames. By contrast, she was a model of stately grace when smiling through those imposing Foundation Day ceremonies at Senate House, and a near-miracle of stamina and resilience at each of the twice-yearly marathons called Presentation Days, long degree-duties in the Royal Albert Hall immediately followed by attendance at services at the Abbey or St. Paul's.

Old hands at the University also remember their most famous

Chancellor, not so much as a lady in official hat and gown, but as a crinolined fairy figure floating expertly round a ballroom floor when she attended Students' Union dances, lighter on her feet than anyone present, and entirely *en rapport* with the young men about her. Youths would take dancing lessons against the possibility of partnering the gossamer lady.

There is the true tale of one nervous young President of the Union who was a ballroom trier, but whose terpsichorean antics suggested that he possessed two left feet. Dutifully taking the floor with the radiant royal figure, he stumbled round in a state of perspiring embarrassment whilst his partner featly avoided kicks on the ankles and smiled as though in the arms of a prince of the waltz. It was a dance which made the boy (who in later years became an M.P. and a Q.C.) a Queen Mum Worshipper for ever, for, in the middle of the bumpy revolutions Her Majesty the Chancellor whispered into his ear: 'Don't worry, Mr. President, you haven't knocked my tiara off yet.' She has always loved dancing.

'Hooked' on Racing

But her renowned enjoyment is horse racing. It was at this time of her life, the Fifties and Sixties, that she had become inextricably 'hooked' (her own word) on this recreation in which her involvement has long been famous. Not, one hastens to add, as a rider but as a breeder and owner of jumping thoroughbreds. The whole Royal Family's enthusiasm for riding is proverbial – Anne, the Princess Royal, is the star of that firmament – and, as well, Queen Elizabeth's own family in Scotland long ago knew all about training racehorses.

Her own years as an owner began in 1949, soon after she had become King George VI's Queen, when one evening at Windsor during an Ascot Week dinner party that superb amateur rider

Opposite The Castle of Mey – the Queen Mother's home in the North on the austere Caithness coast.

Below A hug from a small Prince Charles as his grandmother arrives back in London from her North American tour of 1954. Princess Anne waits her turn. The Queen and all the Royal Family headed the welcome at Waterloo Station.

'over the sticks', the late Lord Mildmay, persuaded her that steeplechasing was more exhilarating than 'the Flat' which was the age-old sport of royalty. Experimentally, she bought a 'chaser', shared it with Princess Elizabeth in fact. Then, on her own, acquired horse after horse, seriously going into the business. So greatly did her enthusiasm and support develop that it is not too much to say that the establishment of National Hunt racing as a major sport is in great measure due to Her Majesty's keenness and knowledge of the 'winter game'.

Early successes included a 'treble' in one day at Lingfield (March 9, 1961) when one of her most famous horses, The Rip, was among the three to be first past the post. At one period she had well over a dozen good class horses in training, and her career as an owner reached peaks in the seasons between 1968 and 1971. Year after year, Major Peter Cazalet, a great friend, trained for her at his lovely home, Fairlawne in West Kent. Since Peter's death in 1973 the Queen Mother's horses have been in the expert charge of Fulke Walwyn at Lambourn in Berkshire. Successes of the last few years have included a victory in the Grand Military Gold Cup at Sandown Park. In March '86 she had another triumph from the same course: three winners in one day. And in the following month came the most important race she has ever won: the Whitbread Gold Cup.

The total number of winners she has owned in all the steeplechasing years is becoming not far short of the 400 mark. Recently, Her Majesty's racing has been on a gentler scale, but she attends meetings when official duties allow – and is even happier in the convivial paddock than in the Royal Box, one

suspects. She is never out of touch with racing events. It is probably true to say that she simply enjoys horses *as* horses – likes to be with her animals just as much as being present to cheer the races themselves. She is never happier than when gum-booting round the stables at Lambourn or visiting the Royal Stud headquarters at Sandringham with sugar in her coat pockets and a bag of carrots in her hands – though what the public see of her mostly is a lady in best clothes, waving excitedly from her viewing-point at a big meeting as the mounts go thundering by.

She doesn't bet. She doesn't strive for financial rewards or go in for commercial selling of a favourite animal when competitive days are done. On the contrary, she 'keeps in touch', and will go and visit a horse as an old friend when it is out at grass in the 'good home' she has found for it.

There is one event in the Queen Mother's racing story which is remembered even by people who do not know a racehorse from a carthorse, such was the drama of the happening, and such the unsolved mystery. The Grand National of 1956 was the occasion – 'The Classic She Should Have Won'. Running in the great event that year was a grand horse of hers named Devon Loch, ridden by the jockey Dick Francis (since those days a world-famous writer of best-selling crime novels). Throughout the gruelling race over the Aintree fences the horse and rider had forged to the fore faultlessly. Then, when six lengths ahead of every remaining runner and only fifty yards from the winning-post, the unbelievable happened. Suddenly and inexplicably, Devon Loch collapsed and lay flat on the turf, legs splayed out, and Francis, helpless beside his horse, stood aghast and in tears.

Above *Always a horse lover, Her Majesty became a regular attender at Badminton's Three Day Event each year. Here she is with her host, the late Duke of Beaufort (right) and some of her own family.*

Below *Queen Elizabeth The Queen Mother in her role as Chancellor of the University of London, an office she energetically held for twenty-five years.*

Left *Her Majesty conferred the Honorary Degree of Doctor of Laws on her Private Secretary, Sir Martin Gilliat on November 24, 1977.*

Below *Having installed Peter Ustinov as Rector of Dundee University on October 20, 1968, the Queen Mother, then Chancellor, enjoys his speech.*

Below *HRH The Prince of Wales accepted an Honorary Degree of Doctor of Laws at London University on November 11, 1974. Here he is hooded by the Queen Mother, as Chancellor.*

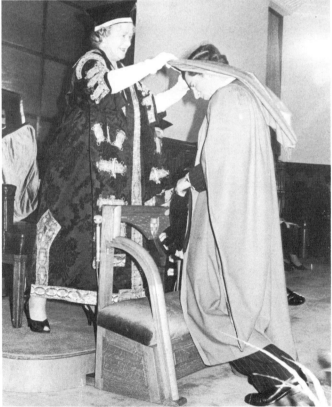

Any owner other than the watching Queen Mother would have been in tears too (the crowds had been yelling their joy at what had seemed a 'cert' as a royal victory for her). But no. Though the cup of triumph had been dashed from her lips, she never turned a hair and was as self-controlled as ever as she turned away to descend from the Royal Box to console the stricken jockey and congratulate the surprised winner. All she said publicly was: 'Well, that's racing.'

Horses! And dogs. Animals have always been part of the image of the Royal Family's domestic, personal life. They possess many dogs of several breeds, but the most popularly known for over half a century have been the stumpy little smooth-coated Welsh corgis, the short-tailed Pembroke breed. Queen Elizabeth has owned and loved generations of them; and she it was who introduced them to the family, (and eventually made the breed nationally known and popular). That was back in 1933, when she was Duchess of York. Her little daughter Elizabeth had seen a friend's corgi pup and fallen in love with it. The Duke, urged by his wife, managed to buy a similar one for the Princess, and it was at once called Dookie, a contraction of 'the Duke of York's puppy'. In modern times, the small dogs are part of the scenery inside Clarence House; and, incidentally, those who work in the house are aware that the pets, though attractive and intelligent, may at times disclose uncertain temper and disagreeable teeth.

But members of Queen Elizabeth's Household, though occasionally they may have nursed a scarred ankle or finger, do not take the menace too seriously: there is cherished in one of the rooms a requested photocopy of a large newspaper headline, printed after a footman allegedly suffered a slight abrasion: 'ROYAL CORGI STRIKES AGAIN!' The dogs are part of Her Majesty's scene, and she knows it. It was a royal smile, not a frown, which greeted the comedian who, parodying Gershwin, suggested there might be a royal opera called 'Corgi and Bess'.

The Sixties

The nineteen-sixties were a decade which began happily enough. There was the birth, in the first February, of Her Majesty's third grandchild, Prince Andrew (the one who, a quarter of a century later, was to marry and take her late

The Royal Family attending the Badminton Horse Trials – a regular date. This was in April 1956. While the Queen uses her cine camera, the Queen Mother and Princess Margaret watch her new horse, Countryman III, take a jump.

husband's ducal style of York). There was that marriage of the second daughter (the Margaret-and-Tony wedding was on a sparkling early Maytime day in '60). And then, soon after those excitements, the Queen Mother enthusiastically undertook one of the longest and most vividly remembered overseas tours of her widowhood life: she was off to the Dark Continent again, a visit to South-East Africa with daily programmes which less energetic people would have found very exhausting. The schedule included extensive travels in Northern Rhodesia and Nyasaland (now Zambia and Malawi), and also the official opening of the vast Kariba Dam on the Zambezi.

But a cruel blow in the next year, 1961: the death of her brother Sir David Bowes-Lyon – David, the other 'Benjamin' of her childhood, who had remained close and dear to his sister throughout all his years and had lived at the old home, St. Paul's Walden. He died, at fifty-nine, whilst on holiday in Scotland at Birkhall, Queen Elizabeth's house on the Balmoral estate; but the funeral was down in England, for David was buried at the Hertfordshire home beside the lawns and enchanted woodlands where he and Elizabeth had played together fifty years before.

That was a sad loss; and inevitably more were to come in following years as relatives, contemporaries and old friends were, in the old saying, 'gathered'. But Her Majesty's griefs have always been deep and private. The public have known her for ever with head held high, keeping up strength and hope and cheer through *new* lives, *new* alliances, *new* additions to the family. She has beamed upon wedding after wedding, birth after birth. One great occasion was the marriage of her nephew, the Duke of Kent, to Miss Katharine Worsley. This, in 1961, brought State pageantry north to York Minster.

Then an event which gave special joy to the Scot in Queen Elizabeth: the wedding in 1963 of the attractive and universally liked young Princess Alexandra of Kent to the Honourable

The Queen Mother studies Lester Piggott riding The Minstrel just before he went to his superb Jubilee Derby victory in 1977.

Angus Ogilvy. The bridegroom was a son of the twelfth Earl of Airlie, for many years the Queen Mother's Lord Chamberlain; and the Airlie family have a long record of service to and close friendship with royalty. (The elder brother of Angus is the Earl of Airlie of today, and Lord Chamberlain.) Angus had proposed to the Princess during one of the Queen Mother's parties at that Scottish 'Birkhall', which is a delightful Queen Anne house beside a Dee tributary, the River Muick – a house which Herself has attractively extended, and which has been not only her own regular Highland hideaway but, through the years, a haven for young honeymooners of her family.

The 'Alex and Angus' marriage strongly appealed to the Queen's sense of history: it linked her family, the Strathmores, to the great patrician Airlie family even more closely than geographical proximity had done through the centuries (for Glamis Castle and the Airlies' castle, Cortachy, near Kirriemuir, are neighbours).

Here's a Health . . .

Whether living in Scotland or England, Queen Elizabeth has throughout her years been what the doctors call 'a good physical specimen'. In lay terms, her strength and vigour, and the tirelessness, have been legendary. Only very occasionally did she cause anxiety. In the Fifties and Sixties one remembers occasional stumbles, a twisted ankle, fractures of a small bone in the foot. From these she made quick recoveries – and continued to wear high heels. In 1964 (the year in which the fourth grandchild Prince Edward was born) she underwent an appendicectomy in London's King Edward VII's Hospital for Officers – and almost immediately afterwards was sitting up and receiving friends, smile in place and face and hair immaculate. The three weeks she spent in the West Indies which was supposed to be a period of rest and convalescence after that operation was in fact spent in sedulous touring. She breezed through twelve of the major Caribbean islands: that was her idea of 'taking it easy'!

Two years later, however, she really was brought to a halt by a serious abdominal operation, in the same London hospital. It was the only major surgery she had ever undergone, and it was

carried out on December 10, 1966 (the date was precisely thirty years after the Abdication which made her a Queen). This time she had to remain in hospital during all that Christmas and New Year season, weeks during which a tide of visiting relatives, telegrams, letters, flowers and a whole variety of 'get well' gifts from people flowed into the hospital. The tributes to the patient would have swamped her room had they not been allowed to embellish also the nearby wards and corridors of 'Sister Agnes's', as this hospital is familiarly known. The area looked like an annexe of Chelsea Flower Show.

The spirit of the patient did not flag even during the many uncomfortable days of recuperation. One afternoon, her bedroom became the excited Royal Box of a racehorse owner as, through B.B.C. television coverage specially rescheduled for her, she watched three of her horses win prizes.

After that hospital experience for a woman of sixty-six, some easing of the pace of life might have been expected; but no, before the spring of 1967 she was out and about again, remarkably recovered, avid for travel. And travel she did, touring in France and, yet again, going to some of her favourite regions of Canada, the Atlantic provinces, including of course the one she likes to pronounce as 'New Scotland' almost as much as its proper name, 'Nova Scotia'.

The next few years were to see her carrying out over two hundred engagements each twelvemonth.

The year 1967 was the one in which there was a public recognition of the Duchess of Windsor by the Queen – and thus, for the Queen Mother too, a brief meeting in London with the woman who had been the key figure in the Abdication over thirty years earlier. The scene was a small stand for spectators, erected in the Mall at the corner of the wall of Marlborough House where there was unveiled a plaque to the memory of Queen Mary. The Queen invited Queen Mary's son the Duke of Windsor, now aged 73, to come to England for the ceremony,

Above *At Royal Ascot in 1976. Behind the Queen Mother is Her Majesty the Queen. Also seen in the photograph are Princess Margaret, the Marquess of Abergavenny (with the umbrella), and to his left Lord Porchester. On the Queen's left is Major W. H. (Dick) Hern.*

Above *At Sandown Park in March 1954 Lieutenant Colonel Blacker bows to the Queen Mother, after she had presented the Grand Military Gold Cup to him for winning the race on Pointsman.*

Above *Mother and daughter in the Royal Box during the 1988 Derby, which was won by the Aga Khan's Kahyasi. Even in the intervals between the events, there is never doubt about Their Majesties' fascination with the scenes on the Epsom Downs racecourse.*

Right *On a busy day of London engagements, the Queen Mother found time to visit the home of the King's Troop, Royal Horse Artillery, famous for salutes of guns and spectacular rides.*

Opposite, bottom *Fishing in the River Dee, with ghillie in attendance. Queen Elizabeth's angling expertise is something she still possesses; she has taught all her grandsons the fisherman's art.*

Left *After the State Funeral of Sir Winston Churchill on January 30, 1965, the Royal Family, Heads of State and leading politicians gather on the steps of St. Paul's.*

Below *Her Majesty arriving with Princess Margaret at the Royal Opera House to attend a Silver Jubilee Gala Performance.*

Opposite *In April 1959 Queen Elizabeth The Queen Mother and Princess Margaret were received by Pope John XXIII at the Vatican. Here they are leaving after their audience with His Holiness.*

Left *Queen Elizabeth has had few ailments and has never allowed mishaps to interfere with her official engagements if at all possible. Here, having cracked a bone in her left foot, she consented to a few moments of travel by wheelchair on arriving at a Newcastle-upon-Tyne waterfront in 1961 to launch a new liner, the 22,000-ton* Northern Star.

Below *When at Sandringham House, the family have always made it their custom to walk to Sunday morning service in the little 'Royal Parish Church' (St. Mary Magdalene) which is within the House's grounds. This snapshot has become a pleasant vintage photograph: it was taken 1969. Prince Charles escorts his grandmother; his brothers are still small boys.*

Opposite *From their earliest days, 'choppers' have been natural conveyances for the Queen Mother. Here she is descending from one of the Royal Navy's helicopters to the deck of HMS* Ark Royal *on a summer day in '58.*

Right *The Garden Room at Clarence House, Her Majesty's London home – one of the pictures taken specially at Queen Elizabeth's homes. An unfinished portrait of the Queen Mother, by Augustus John, hangs over the fireplace.*

Right *On the walls of the ground floor Corridor at Clarence House hang many pictures of the racehorses of the Queen Mother's forebears. The large picture is of Coerstone, winner of the Derby and the 2,000 Guineas in 1843, and owned by Mr John Bowes. Top right is Coerstone's sire, Touchstone, with a stable lad. Below is a Stubbs painting of one of the Bowes's bay ponies.*

Left *The lovely first floor Drawing Room at Clarence House. The group portrait on the right is of the Misses Cavendish-Bentinck, one of whom was Queen Elizabeth's mother.*

Below *At the other end of the Drawing Room is a rare William-and-Mary lacquered cabinet on a silvered stand.*

Duke of Gloucester, who had been an invalid for some years, died. Thus Prince Richard, the remaining son, came to be Duke at the age of thirty. (Today, a family man, he is one of the most informal of royal persons, chugging away from Kensington Palace on a small motorbike to work in the City, his spacemen-like crash helmet completing the desired anonymity.)

None of the clan is anonymous to the Queen Mother, of course. She does not have to turn to her birthday-book for names and arrival dates and then, in time, the appearances of offspring on the scene. They are all in her mind and memory; and it has always been her way to concentrate, not on the demise of old relatives but on the arrivals and adventures of new ones, on the joys rather than the sadnesses of her recent decades – the happy anniversaries and popular celebrations. So it was that she thoroughly savoured the 1972 silver wedding ceremonies of her reigning daughter, the Queen (twenty-four years after her own silver wedding). There was a thanksgiving service at St. Paul's; and in the carriage processions through the streets of London she rode ahead of the Sovereign's state landau in a coach which drew loud cheers all the way: Her Majesty had two young grandsons sitting opposite to her – Prince Andrew and Prince Edward, both good-looking and greatly enjoying themselves.

Then, in 1973, the marriage of her granddaughter Princess Anne (the much-admired Princess Royal now) to a masterly horseman, the swift and cheerful and remarkably inarticulate Captain Mark Phillips. Incidentally, the bride's name in the register is 'Anne Mountbatten-Windsor'.

Three years later came celebrations which the Queen Mother specially remembers, though they belonged to her daughter rather than to herself: the Queen's fiftieth birthday parties. Next, 1977 had its special mark in Royal Family history when a long series of celebrations studded the twenty-fifth anniversary of Queen Elizabeth the Second, whose mother took delight in the Silver Jubilee events as much as anyone in the land.

A particular pleasure of '77 was the arrival of the Jubilee Year Royal Baby, the son – christened Peter Mark Andrew and, at his mother's resolve, bearing no royal title – who was born to Princess Anne and Captain Phillips on November 15, four years and a day after their wedding. Here was the first of a new generation of the Royal Family. The birth of Peter Phillips made the Queen a grandmother at the age of fifty-one and brought to Queen Elizabeth The Queen Mother her latest style – Great-Grannie. He was to be followed by the others of the latest generation who are now rapidly growing up: Zara Anne Elizabeth, Princess Anne's second child, born in 1981; cousin Prince William of Wales, Prince Charles's important first son – second in the line of Succession to the Throne – little more than twelve months later; and brother Prince Harry, born in the late summer of 1984.

Those were family events. In Her Majesty's public life, one of the notable events as the Seventies drew to a close – she described it as 'one of the happiest days of all my life' – was her installation as Lord Warden and Admiral of the Cinque Ports, a ceremony which took place on August 1, 1979, in Dover. It was not only a happy event but an historic salute. It was South-East England's 'invasion coast' honouring a royal champion's conspicuous service to Crown and country. This unique Warden post is an honorary office now, but in olden days it meant a command of vital importance: Guardian and Defender of the ports, and their fleets, which were bulwarks of the Realm. The Ports, a confederation of coastal towns, probably date from Roman times, and certainly as an organization can be traced back to the days of William the Conqueror. Winston Churchill was one of those who were proud to occupy the Warden office in the twentieth century; and by that measure, plus the fact that no royal person and no woman of any kind had ever had the title bestowed before, the appointment was signal acknowledgement of the Queen Mother's suitability and stature.

On the actual installation day the Kent coast was memorable for most unkind deluges of rain, but the weather failed to extinguish Her Majesty's shine and smile, or the full-dress processions and gun salutes and musical tributes as she was duly created 'Constable of Dover Castle and Lord Warden and Admiral of the Cinque Ports', to the delight of people in the original 'antient towns' of Hastings, New Romney, Hythe, Dover and Sandwich – the original five – and the other places including Deal and Folkestone which have been added to the association through the years.

It was typical of this Lord Warden that, a day of high ceremonial though this was, she took with her, to make it a family occasion too, three grandchildren: Prince Edward, and Lord Linley and Lady Sarah Armstrong-Jones (Princess Margaret's son and daughter). They all had a marvellous time, sailing to Dover in the Royal Yacht Britannia and then the youngsters watching Grannie being an Admiral and swearing 'to maintain the franchises, liberties, customs and usages of the ports'.

Since that day she has been arduous in making visits to her Kent and Sussex 'realms'. And, being a person who cannot bear to miss a 'date' if she can possibly help it, she demonstrated remarkable perseverence in getting to the coast one morning a couple of years later. She was off to a series of Cinque Ports engagements in Kent when her helicopter had to make an emergency landing and decant her on to the grass in the middle of Windsor Great Park. She wasn't frightened; she was furious – and marched off with her secretary to find a small fixed-wing aircraft to give her a lift. Having thus, a bit late, managed her journey to the sea, one would have thought that a lady who was then eighty-one would have been slightly unnerved. But not this lady (to whom helicopters are a perfectly natural way of getting around). She unhesitatingly hopped into another 'chopper' in Kent to carry on and catch up with her string of engagements that same long day.

During the Lord Warden year, 1979, Queen Elizabeth had been busy almost every month. She was in Canada yet again – Toronto and Halifax – sailing energetically through official routines at which other royals, even the young ones, would have quailed.

Media-people who were covering that trip have a special recall of one of her remarks. She was in Halifax, Nova Scotia, just after the historic General Election result, back in the United Kingdom, which brought Mrs. Margaret Thatcher to the beginning of her long political reign at Number Ten Downing Street as leader of the Government. Britain had a woman Prime Minister for the first time ever, and it was headline news all over the world. It so happened that an informal gathering in Nova Scotia gave reporters an opportunity to have a word with the

Opposite In the Royal Box at Covent Garden on June 21, 1966, to attend a Gala performance in aid of the Opera House's Benevolent Fund.

Right *The gardens at Birkhall are largely the creation of Queen Elizabeth. Here is a view of the side entrance.*

Below *This unique photograph gives Birkhall a jewel-like appearance against a majestic Scottish backcloth. Birkhall is Her Majesty's Aberdeenshire home.*

Opposite *Balmoral Castle. Still a loved retreat for all the Royal Family is the 'dear Paradise' which Prince Albert and Queen Victoria built beneath the Grampian hills. The castle is seen here with its turrets caught by the setting sun.*

Queen Mother. The question they all asked of Her Majesty was: 'Do you think that the fact of a female becoming Premier will make a great difference to women in your country, Ma'am?' The reply was: 'No. Not a bit, not at all.' Then, as the news corps were putting their notebooks away, one of those special twinkles came into the Queen's eye, and she added: 'It's going to have a big effect on the *men*.'

Canada, as ever, gave glad memories. But that same year, as another decade was ending, brought shock and sorrow. On the August Bank Holiday Monday, Earl Mountbatten, the Royal Family's 'Uncle Dickie' and elder statesman who was almost exactly the same age as Queen Elizabeth, was coldbloodedly murdered by an Irish terrorist's bomb placed in his boat near his holiday house in County Sligo. Her Majesty characteristically showed little outward sign of what must have been sharpest shock and grief.

It was left to the Prince of Wales, at the Mountbatten memorial service in St. Paul's, poignantly to express the family's deep bereavement and horror. To a hushed congregation, he spoke with a rare public anger of the 'mindless cruelty' of the killers and of the 'vulnerability of civilised democracy and freedom to the kind of subhuman extremism which blows people up when it feels like it'.

The words were memorably emotive. It might have been the Prince's grandmother speaking. She and all her family were in the Cathedral's congregation, intently hearing and intensely feeling the emotions that were being expressed. They were, surely, Queen Elizabeth's own sentiments too. But it has always been her way that deep personal reactions, many and fierce though they may be, are not broadcast. She is a natural talker, most sincere and charming in conversation, eloquent too in expressions of face and gestures of hands, but in innate

Opposite *The massive 100-foot tower which dominates the granite grandeur of Royal Balmoral.*

sensitivities she is very much a private person also. She possesses one of the most agreeable voices in the Royal Family, but when it comes to voicing an address in public, then the occasion is not one for putting personal and severe reactions on parade. She bears losses with fortitude – *in public*. But in private she has, too often, been sorely stricken.

Her family know her character and her views, and her influence is considerable. In the years ahead historians may well say that the powerful role she has played in the history of both her own folk and the nation to whom she has been for so long a mother figure has been effective through 'keeping quiet but setting example'. Perhaps it may be that the amount of her importance is in inverse ratio to the amount of her speech-making! Friends have said that her *silences* are immensely eloquent.

Certainly the totals of her formal speeches are no measure of her active involvement in national life. She is patron or president of over three hundred organizations, Colonel-in-Chief of a dozen regiments. She is head of orders of chivalry, holder of numerous honorary degrees, and a Master of the Bench of the Middle Temple. A quick trawl through the lists of hospitals, schools, charities and assorted societies which have her official patronage (and patronage by personal gifts too) brings wide variety to the surface, disclosing, for instance, the Bible Reading Fellowship, the College of Speech Therapists, the British Home and Hospital for Incurables, the Grand Military Race Meeting, the Injured Jockeys Fund, the National Trust, the Royal School of Needlework, the Dachshund Club, the Keep Britain Tidy Group, and membership of Women's Institutes and guilds of the like in towns and many rural reaches, always including Windsor and Sandringham, Crathie and Birkhall.

Such is the official, the publicly-reported side of her activities and offices and benefactions. The other side of her life – the work she does for friends and her own folk, for her staffs and their families, the help given to rural communities and cottages widespread – remains unsung behind the private shield of 'holidays' spent for certain months every year in rural Berkshire and Norfolk, and in the hinterlands of Grampian and Highland.

CHAPTER NINE

FLOWER OF THE FAMILY

ALL THE LATE Seventies and Eighties saw Queen Elizabeth regularly 'in the news' somewhere or other.

Even though she is not annoyingly pursued by the Press, as some of the others are, during her regular private times spent in the countryside of England or Scotland or occasionally in northern Europe – the weeks which are free of public engagements – it remains true that hardly a week goes by without the publication of some pictures or stories about 'the Golden Grannie'. The spotlights play most persistently nowadays on the young ones of the family, but public interest in the Queen Mother never ceases. She herself does not cultivate an 'image', and the word has no meaning to her. Should she try to answer questions about it, there would come simply an echo of something said many years ago: 'I just want to go on being myself to the best of my ability.'

Nevertheless, hers, the longest-running of royal fan clubs, is firmly rooted in Fleet Street. News of her is always wanted, always has been. The more experienced a cameraman or reporter, the more likely he is to class her the lasting Flower of the Family. The best-liked, the most productive.

Some of the stories of the fun and freshness of her first emerged out of newspaper columns. For instance, the long-ago 'leak' from a room where Her Majesty was informal host to a group of people who were chatting and at the same time turning casually to the television set in a corner. A public event was being relayed through 'the Box', and presently the strains of the National Anthem were heard. 'Oh, do switch the set off,' said the royal hostess. 'Unless one is actually there, it's rather out of place and embarrassing, don't you think? Rather like hearing the Lord's Prayer whilst playing canasta.'

Queen Elizabeth does not make television appearances – not for television's sake. She does not give interviews. But her public occasions are a different story, because nobody realizes better than she does the difficulties of the news cameramen's job. No photographer herself, yet she knows where the favourite shots may be possible as she goes on her rounds. And so, of course, a

mutual respect is engendered. And good pictures are the result.

Who else, on a hospital visit, would turn back to the bedside of someone 'in the news' because she had noticed that one unfortunate man among the photographers hadn't quite loaded a film in time when she had first stopped at the bed? Who else pause and give a second (a 'when you're ready') pat on the head to a dog because she had heard a cameraman's curse muttered over a jammed shutter during her first encounter with the animal? And who but she would have said to a self-important little Town Hall fusspot who had been trying to shoo a veteran Fleet Street newsman away from the red carpet: 'Please don't do that. Mr. Devon and I are old friends and we both have our work to do.'

This is not to suggest that the lady is a posturing show-off. If, as has been suggested, she is the finest actress of the entire clan, then it is but performing naturally: acting herself.

The whole Royal Family, media targets, have learned from her, and thankfully give her their support. Some of them are 'naturals' in their own right, whilst others, perhaps nervous, find their exposure trying when the massed flash-bulbs of the Press seem to be forever popping. But in one way or another, some imprint of the Queen Mother is on them all as they face publicity.

She, the Eminent Victorian who has 'seen it all', has shown to her kin the need for adaptability and the path of change. The Windsors are a close-knit family, and the complete picture of Her Majesty is in a setting of them, a large collection in these days. For marriage partnerships develop and hold firm (to quote the words of the present Queen on her own Silver Wedding anniversary) 'in the web of family relationships between parents and children, grandparents and grandchildren, between cousins, aunts and uncles'. There are now eight decades of people between the royal great-grandmother and the princes William and Harry and their new generation.

It is worthwhile to take a look at some of the human beings and relationships in the web which the Queen Mother holds together.

The qualities which she has given to her reigning daughter, now the most experienced Head of State in the world, need no rehearsing. That the Second Elizabeth is a monarch of rare merit owes much to the exemplary upbringing and counsel given by

Opposite Her Majesty, with the traditional nosegay, leaves Westminster Abbey at the head of the Royal Almonry procession, after the Royal Maundy service and distribution of alms in 1970.

Above *Princess Margaret rides out with her mother from Buckingham Palace, to witness the Trooping the Colour ceremony of June 1981 – the Sovereign's Birthday spectacle on Horse Guards Parade.*

Left *The Princess Royal and her husband, Captain Mark Phillips, with their children: a snapshot taken soon after Zara's birth.*

Opposite *The youngest royal generation comes into the picture (and enjoys it!). It is September 1987. The Prince and Princess of Wales are taking their small second son, Prince Harry, to his first day at a nursery school in Kensington. Prince William insists on getting into the act too by waving good luck to his younger brother.*

Viscount Linley (left), Princess Margaret's son – now a craftsman in wood – admires another artist's creation.

her mother, especially just before and during the early days of the reign – and maybe also to the exchanges of views which only today's private line out of Clarence House knows.

Even Queen Elizabeth's quick and confident Mountbatten son-in-law, Prince Philip, has often enjoyed the considerable backing of the Queen Mother as he pursues his many-sided and often provocative role in the national life. Just as a Queen Dowager has no constitutional position whatever, the Duke of Edinburgh, as husband of a Queen Regnant, has no business with the affairs of state. His chief service for over thirty years has been strong personal support for his wife in many of her duties and decisions; and meanwhile, from the start, he has made a busy public life for himself as an indefatigable stimulator of progress in science and technology, wildlife preservation and all-round training for the more promising types of the world's young people. One thing Prince Philip enjoys is meeting people (providing there is no genuflexion!), and in that aptitude he is an echo of his mother-in-law, whose talent for public encounters he admires. It is when he bluntly 'airs his views' that he is the antithesis of Queen Elizabeth.

As to Prince Charles, the intimate rapport which exists between the Prince of Wales and his grandmother is well known as a bond of strong affection. Her love and comfort lit a lifelong glow in his heart in the early and lonely years when he was far away at Gordonstoun School; and no one exceeds the Queen Mother in sympathetic understanding of the present crusading nature and preoccupations – and the trauma – of this caring King-to-Be: his philosopher's anxieties over the plight of young unemployed people, for instance, and his concern as to how, without becoming a politician, he can cause something practical to be done about it.

Two generations apart, Queen Mother and first grandson are much alike – even, for instance, in enjoying such diverse relaxations as country solitudes and 'Crazy Gang' comedies. Each has a strictly resolute character, but leavened by a darting sense of fun.

When Prince Charles at last acquired a wife (the story is told in the next chapter) there began the 'Diana link' with Clarence House. Queen Elizabeth's remembered experience of coming fresh into the Royal Family, albeit sixty years before, was something which was well told and which sustained the new Princess of Wales when she was 'learning the ropes' and living at the Queen Mother's house in the early betrothal weeks. Grannie was a strength and refuge. And still is.

Her Majesty, not unnaturally, has a particular pride in her only granddaughter, Anne, the Princess Royal, who has

Left *Princess Anne made a hazardous tour of African and Middle Eastern countries in 1982, as President of The Save the Children Fund – a mission which appealed to her grandmother's heart. Here she is at a welfare centre in a war-torn Beirut, Lebanon.*

Opposite, top *December 22, 1977. Five generations at the Buckingham Palace christening of Peter, Princess Anne's infant son – the eldest being the late Princess Alice, Countess of Athlone (seated beside Princess Anne), a grandchild of Queen Victoria. The paternal grandparents, Mr and Mrs Peter Phillips, are on the left.*

Opposite, bottom *Youngest grandson Prince Edward shares in the senior patron's enjoyment of the 1982 Badminton Horse Trials.*

Opposite *The indefatigable,
frequently uncomfortable, tours of
Anne, the Princess Royal, as
President of The Save the
Children Fund, have aroused
widespread respect for Her Royal
Highness in recent years. Here,
she is 'seeing for herself' in
Uganda, 1988.*

Top *Celebrating her seventy-fifth
birthday on August 4, 1975 at
Royal Lodge. Prince Andrew, on
the right, has just presented a gift
of two pottery dishes he had made
at Gordonstoun, his school.*

Right *The young King of
Sweden, Carl XVI Gustav, with
Queen Elizabeth The Queen
Mother and the late Earl
Mountbatten of Burma.*

Above *On the day of the
Eightieth Birthday Thanksgiving
Service, the Queen Mother, back
at the Palace, gathered her six
grandchildren about her for this
photograph. Standing, from the
left, are Viscount Linley, Prince
Andrew, the Prince of Wales and
Prince Edward. On Her
Majesty's left is the Princess
Royal, and Lady Sarah
Armstrong-Jones sits at her other
side.*

Right *Gala smiles match the
gala ballet staged at Covent
Garden on the evening of Queen
Elizabeth's Eightieth Birthday.
She took her whole family to the
Opera House. Here, in the Royal
Box, Princess Margaret is beside
her mother.*

Above *Although her life is full of ceremonial engagements and charity work, the Princess Royal continues to be involved in equestrian activities and sometimes also appears as a racecourse jockey.* Right *The Princess is also a diligent parent, and a trainer too, passing on her equestrian skill to her daughter Zara Phillips.*

inherited Queen Elizabeth's hard-working character, straight-talking common sense, and zest for life. The pony-riding girl has become a world figure, and by no means only when she herself is on horseback. The metamorphosis of the once hard-riding, hard-slanging horsewoman who used to be savaged by the newspaper gossip columns for her treatment of media men is one of the most striking transformations of recent years. The dedicated journeys of investigation into deprived and dangerous regions of the Third World, in the cause of the children's charities which she heads, have roused widespread admiration. She has drawn astonished approval even from people wont to prate that they 'have no use for the Royals'; and the fact is that in recent years this princess has tirelessly fulfilled far more official engagements, undertaken far more long journeys, than anyone in the family, the Queen included.

And, as to the media pendulum, it has swung ninety degrees and points with an exceptional fondness to Her Royal Highness. She is hailed almost as a latter-day Florence Nightingale and an exalted Mother Teresa rolled into one.

Prince Andrew, grandson number two, the most robustly self-confident and lively of the Buckingham Palace family, whose marriage brought another Duchess of York to the royal scene, as a serving officer carries on the naval career tradition which meant a great deal to the Queen Mother's husband; and Andrew stands high in her affection for that and for much else.

Above *From the balcony of Buckingham Palace the Queen and her family wave to the thousands who have come to see them on Jubilee Day, 1977. (*FROM THE LEFT*) Prince Charles, Prince Edward, Prince Andrew, the late Earl Mountbatten, the Queen, Prince Philip, Captain Mark Phillips, Princess Anne, the Queen Mother and Princess Margaret.*

Right *In the Silver Jubilee procession back from St. Paul's to the Palace, Queen Elizabeth The Queen Mother rode with three grandsons. Uniformed Prince Charles has his Welsh Guards bearskin on his head.*

Opposite *Princess Anne had married Captain Mark Phillips in November 1973. This was the brilliant wedding scene in Westminster Abbey. The bride's two attendants were nine year olds: Lady Sarah Armstrong-Jones and (in the kilt) Prince Edward.*

As to Prince Edward, the youngest grandson prince, something of a loner, he is the one who *broke* a tradition (the custom that male offspring of the Sovereign enter one of the uniformed Services) by controversially resigning from the Royal Marines soon after his plucky full-time entry into the Corps. Then, having become a civilian, he again made an unprecedented move in 1988 by taking a paid job in the commercial theatre – a step which must have commanded his grandmother's particular sympathy and hope. She has always understood Edward's leaning towards the performing arts, and remembers how, when she took him – at barely six years old – to a concert he was both fascinated and very self-contained. Her Majesty said later: 'I knew he'd like it, but I've never known a boy sit so still.'

There remains, in this roll-call of principal royal people, the Queen Mother's second daughter, Princess Margaret, now middle-aged, the aunt of Charles and Anne, Andrew and Edward. She has faded from the forefront of the Palace scene where once she shone. In the years since her marriage was dissolved in 1978, she has gone through periods of trouble in her physical health and occasionally her unconventional private

activities. She has endured hostility in Press reporting, but now is seen, as a busy patron, undertaking public engagements again, and most winningly. Her Royal Highness, in fact, nowadays carries out, with renewed enthusiasm, a variety of official duties connected with the charities for which she works and the regiments of which she is Colonel-in-Chief.

Through the years, it has been a misfortune that this mercurial sister of Queen Elizabeth the Second, a sister socially and artistically talented well above the average, has inevitably had to be the 'also ran' Second Princess in the centre of the monarchy, possessing no obvious constitutional role. Difficulties and criticisms have been heaped upon a highly spirited personality. In calm and quiet waters now, at Kensington Palace, she is fortunate to enjoy the affection and often the company of her two children, and her mother's unfailing understanding. The two, Princess and Queen Mother, have a number of strong fellow-feelings. Upsets and years of sadnesses notwithstanding, mother and daughter remain in harmony. Certainly Her Royal Highness's warmth and spontaneity can strikingly reflect parental character.

The 'minor royals' – it is a phrase *they* use, but Queen

Servants of the Crown

It is not improper to add some of the monarchy's chief officials, the men behind the Throne, to the catalogue of royalty. However firmly the line is drawn between the princes and princesses and those who are in their employ, the fact remains that most of the principal Servants of the Crown are persons of some prominence in the Windsor picture. Day in and day out, their business makes the wheels of constitutional monarchy go round. Moreover, most of these indispensable professionals, who are in paid positions and arcane only in their titles, are close associates and trusted friends of the Highnesses who make up the Royal Firm.

As Her Majesty and her descendants moved with the times through the late Seventies and Eighties, and were publicized more than ever, inescapably the names of certain of the officials of royal Households – not only the Press Secretaries – kept coming into the royal stories. This was usually because of journalistic ferreting, for no covey of workers is more bent upon keeping a low profile than these extremely able backroom boys, the royal functionaries who 'run the shop'.

The Queen Mother knows almost all of them, even the relatively new Palace hands. They are, at times, *her* staff too, for she may be called upon to act as one of the Counsellors of State, taking investitures and receiving ambassadors in the Sovereign's stead, when her daughter is absent from base on overseas tours.

The Lord Chamberlain (Lord Airlie) must be classed the Queen's senior servant, the 'managing director' of the royal household. He and his large department's Comptroller and staff

Above The scene in St. Paul's Cathedral during the service held on June 7, 1977, on the occasion of the Silver Jubilee of Her Majesty The Queen. Standing beside the Queen is the Duke of Edinburgh. On either side of the aisle, the Queen Mother and the Prince of Wales are at the centre of the distinguished congregation's Royal front row.

Opposite The Queen Mother leaving St. Paul's Cathedral after the Silver Jubilee Thanksgiving Service. With her, as she waves in greeting, are Prince Charles (right) and the Princes Andrew and Edward (left).

are acknowledged by anyone who has business with them as the world's most expert organizers of great occasions, the weddings, the State Visits, garden parties, and all manner of ceremonial. Even the posts of Poet Laureate and, so different, the appointment of the Keeper of the Queen's Swans are under the great umbrella of the Lord Chamberlain's Office.

The key figure, however, and the link between the Sovereign and Government, is the Private Secretary. The present one is a gifted Australian named Sir William Heseltine. Incisive, urbane, unflappable, in closest touch with the Queen, Bill Heseltine is in practice the number one courtier.

The Master of the Household is the officer who runs the people who run the palaces, that whole range of workers from the dignified stewards to the 'dailies' with the vacuum-cleaners, the lordly table-deckers to the lowlies of the linen pantries, the pages and the footmen – and even the kitchen people and the

important man who is Royal Pastry Chef.

One of the Master's equals, head of another department, is the royal treasurer; and he is called Keeper of the Privy Purse. Then there is the Mistress of the Robes and the other ladies-in-waiting. They are the Queen's personal friends. So is the Master of the Horse and, particularly, that master's executive officer, the Crown Equerry. He has charge not only of the Royal Mews but every form of transport from high-powered cars to horse-drawn coaches. Such main persons 'around the Throne' are executives in positions of great trust.

But of course the particular Servants of Royalty who are requisite support and background of the *Queen Mother's* story are Her Majesty's own and separate Household whose headquarters are her home at St. James's, a kingdom of its own: Clarence House. As visitors to the House cannot but know, the principal figure encountered there, his employer's chief executive, right hand, and friend, is Lieutenant-Colonel Sir Martin Gilliat, doyen of the courtiers of this and all the Households, a tall, engaging bachelor, ever-welcoming, incessantly busy in the job he loves, utterly devoted to his perennial chief.

The Comptroller of the Household is Captain Sir Alastair Aird (whose wife is a lady-in-waiting to Princess Margaret); Major John Griffin is the Press Secretary, with experience stretching back further than any of his kind; the Lord Chamberlain is the Earl of Dalhousie; the house's Treasurer is Major Sir Ralph Anstruther; and a distinguished and long-serving lady-in-waiting is the Dowager Lady Fermoy (the maternal grandmother of the Princess of Wales), who has been a particular friend of Queen Elizabeth ever since her marriage. Lady Fermoy is herself a charmer, and is a very busy person even during the periods when it is not her turn to be 'in waiting'. She is

Above One of the century's most delightful camera portraits of a mother and her daughter. The camera artistry of Norman Parkinson.

Opposite The Queen Mother leaves St. Paul's Cathedral on Jubilee Day escorted by the Prince of Wales in full dress uniform as Colonel of the Welsh Guards, and followed by Prince Andrew and the then young Prince Edward.

an artist, a musician of talent and organizing ability, and concerned with all manner of activities in London. But she is perhaps most notably associated with the King's Lynn Festival of Music and the Arts which she runs each summer – an event to which Queen Elizabeth always looks forward and enthusiastically attends. Ruth Fermoy is part of the Royal Norfolk scene – but proudly hails from Aberdeenshire. Among other 'Ladies of the Bedchamber' and 'Women of the Bedchamber' also, strong lines of descent from the North are to be discerned.

Even from a mere recital of the names of the key figures at Clarence House it is clear that the onetime Elizabeth Bowes-Lyon still rejoices in having a wealth of Scots around her! And only in the more recent years has there ceased the custom of having the Queen Mother's own Highland Piper marching up and down, a-blowing lustily, in the garden beneath the royal windows at an early hour each morning. In present times, the uniformed piper plays only on celebration days, such as Her Majesty's birthday.

Well before the 1979 birthday came and went, it was clear that the *next* anniversary – the eightieth – was going to be far more than a one-day event.

Above *The working Queen Mother, here seen at her desk at Clarence House in London.*

CHAPTER TEN

THE EMINENT EIGHTIES

ALL THE Queen Mother's birthdays are special, but the eightieth was extra-special. By the time that particular fourth of August arrived – August 1980 of course – it seemed as though we had already been living with the golden milestone for months and months. And indeed the saluting of it had been long planned. Nor were the preliminaries secret. Week after week, well before The Day, assorted tributes were pouring into Clarence House, and, as time went on, the augmented staff were near submerged beneath avalanches of flowers and letters and greetings cards. Presents arrived from all over the world.

Even the main official happening to mark the event, a huge Service of Thanksgiving in St. Paul's Cathedral, anticipated August 4 by three weeks: it took place on July 15.

Had the manner of celebration been left to the decision of the lady herself, she would no doubt have asked for no inordinate or expensive fuss, though certainly prayers of thankfulness and a family gathering. But other ideas overwhelmingly prevailed, so that there was national pageantry and personal parties, both. The fifteenth of July produced resounding pageantry in a gift-wrapped London, its beflagged sidewalks and roadways chock-a-block with people of all ages, anxious to cheer and wave to a special person as she rode by in a state landau, with the Prince of Wales sitting beside her, on her way through Westminster and the City up to Wren's great church at the top of Ludgate Hill.

There was no mistaking that it was Grannie's Day. The Queen had seen to it that, in all the processions, her mother had first place – even over herself, the Monarch. So all the Family were already in church, waiting, when the star of the occasion came. A spectacular-enough stream of escorted horse-drawn carriages had conveyed them: the Queen and Prince Philip, Princess Margaret, Prince Andrew, Prince Edward, the royal Gloucesters and Kents and their children. But when Queen Elizabeth made her special progress along the processional route, her open carriage, accompanied by mounted troopers in full dress uniform of shining cuirasses and brilliantly plumed helmets, the Household Cavalry were a complete *Sovereign's*

Opposite Arriving at the Theatre Royal, Drury Lane – it was Birthday Evening, 1982 – to see 'The Pirates of Penzance'.

Escort, the extra touch normally given only to the *reigning* Queen. For it was the Queen *Mother* who was reigning again, in the hearts and minds of everyone on that day.

And it was the daughter, the Second Elizabeth, who was outside waiting on the steps of St. Paul's to greet her mother on arrival – and then to step into the background, smilingly accepting second place, as the Queen Mother stood waving to the people massed and cheering in front of the cathedral. She made a memorable picture, dressed in the style the world knew and hoped for, smiling from a mist of ostrich feathers and sapphire chiffon. Her dress had diaphanous floating panels on the sleeves which streamed out like banners as she waved, defiantly bare-armed on a day that was lacking in any summer warmth and had in fact sent many people into wearing overcoats. But there she was, on parade and completely in character, impervious to cold winds, belying her years – and loving every minute of it.

Inside the church, all the great personages of realm and Commonwealth were assembled, resplendent lords and ladies, famous officers of state and captains of arms: a star-studded congregation of 2,700 people. But not everybody there was a 'big name': Her Majesty had seen to that, and had done it by applying her own hand to the guest-list and making sure that invitations to the service went to a good many persons who, whilst not publicly known, had been in her service and become her friends. Thus one noticed – all well placed with seats in the transepts – retired garden labourers from Windsor and far Balmoral, former footmen, nurserymaids of bygone years, cooks and pages still in royal service, secretaries and chauffeurs – and her present staff: everyone, indeed, with ten years' service or more. Queen Elizabeth had even found, and arranged her special transporting to the cathedral, an old lady who half a century before had been the cook at 145 Piccadilly when Her Majesty was Duchess of York.

If the nation wanted the thanksgiving service to be *her* day, then, however grand the assembly, she wished to be sure that her friends, high or low, were present. And as she, central figure of it all, walked through the crowded nave she positively glowed, and her smile came like a wave ahead of her. As she passed, you felt that the look she gave was personally for *you*.

The Archbishop of Canterbury, Dr. Runcie, got it right when

Opposite *The Lady of Clarence House surrounded by flowers and books in the privacy of her London home.*

Above *The Lord Mayor of London escorts the Queen Mother up the steps of St. Paul's for the great Birthday Service of 1980. Prince Charles is in attendance.*

in his address he said: 'Royalty puts a human face on the operations of Government; and the Queen Mother helps us to feel that being a citizen of this country is not just being an entry on a central computer, but is being a member of a family. . . . It is difficult to fall in love with committees or policies, but she has shown a human face which has called out affection and loyalty and the sense of *belonging*, without which a nation loses its heart.'

The nation unambiguously lost its heart when the birthday anniversary itself came, on August 4, 1980, and the crowds engulfed Clarence House whilst the Guards marched past playing 'Happy Birthday' with their fifes and drums. The cheers were so loud that it was hard to hear the booming salutes of guns from batteries in Hyde Park and at the Tower of London.

That night – as festive bonfires blazed on Kent and Sussex coasts which were 'hers' as Lord Warden of the Cinque Ports –

Above *The girl who became Princess of Wales. An album snap of very young Lady Diana Spencer holidaying on a Sussex beach. It was 1970.*

Opposite *Now it is July 1981 and the wedding of the Heir to the Throne. Dr. Runcie, the Archbishop of Canterbury, blesses the bride and groom at the marriage service in St. Paul's Cathedral.*

the lady herself went with her family to the Royal Opera House, Covent Garden, to receive the honour of a triple-bill ballet performance. When the grand finale of the gala evening came, silver petals rained down from the theatre ceiling, and performers and audience joined in spontaneous musical salutes to ballet's Number One Patron.

Opposite *The Prince and Princess of Wales drive down Ludgate Hill after their marriage.*

Right *Prince Charles kisses his bride's hand, a romantic gesture before the crowds demanded a 'real' kiss.*

Prince Charles's Marriage

For the Christmas season of that year, Queen Elizabeth was a centre of the customary gathering of all the generations of the royal house at Windsor and, for the New Year, at Sandringham. She was happy herself; she was wishing settled happiness for those around her, and it is tempting to think that her first grandson was much in her mind. Prince Charles was in his thirty-second year of age, the world's most eligible bachelor. The Press was in a crescendo of speculation on who he might marry.

There was not much longer to wait and hope, for early in 1981 the official word came that Britain was to have a Princess of Wales again.

The news broke dramatically in a moment of perfect theatre within Buckingham Palace itself. At eleven o'clock on the morning of February 24, 1981, Queen Elizabeth the Second had just arrived at the dais in the ballroom, ready to carry out an investiture. She stood beneath the lights, a smiling figure in the centre of her courtiers, facing an audience composed of relatives of those she was due to honour. But instead of starting the ceremony she nodded to her Lord Chamberlain (it was Lord Maclean then), who stepped forward, took a deep breath, and read the following statement to the hushed guests:

'The Queen has asked me to let you know that an announcement is being made at this moment in the following terms:

"It is with the greatest pleasure that the Queen and the Duke of Edinburgh announce the betrothal of their beloved son, the Prince of Wales, to the Lady Diana Spencer, daughter of the Earl Spencer and the Honourable Mrs. Shand-Kydd."'

Applause burst out; the Guards orchestra in the minstrels' gallery struck up a lively tune; and Her Majesty began the investiture. Simultaneously, the words of the statement, plus the news that the engagement would be followed by a wedding in July, was being flashed round the world.

The world was already familiar with the fiancée's name. She was 'Lady Di' as far as the tabloid newspapers were concerned, and cameramen and gossip-column writers had been hot on her trail since the previous autumn, noting her in the company of the Heir to the Throne several times, and themselves betting that 'this was the one for Charles'. Yet they weren't sure until that investiture morning.

Until a few months before, this young lady, aged only nineteen, had never been anywhere near the public gaze. But now, as papers and magazines excitedly disclosed the history and the face of 'a lovely English rose', it suddenly seemed extraordinary that His Royal Highness had ever looked at other girls. She'd been under his nose for some years: he was marrying 'the girl next door'. She had spent her childhood years with Park House as her home: it was her parents' house and it was on the

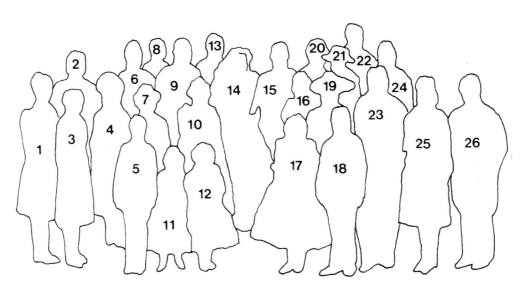

Key to pages 154 and 155 *The full family group posed for the camera in Buckingham Palace on the Great Wedding Day of July 1981. Present are: 1. Princess Anne; 2. Captain Mark Phillips; 3. Princess Margaret; 4. Queen Elizabeth The Queen Mother; 5. Edward van Cutsem; 6. Prince Andrew; 7. The Queen; 8. Viscount Linley; 9. Prince Philip; 10. India Hicks; 11. Clementine Hambro; 12. Catherine Cameron; 13. Prince Edward; 14. The Princess of Wales; 15. The Prince of Wales; 16. Lady Sarah Armstrong-Jones; 17. Sarah Jane Gaselee; 18. Lord Nicholas Windsor; 19. the Hon. Mrs. Frances Shand Kydd; 20. Ruth, Lady Fermoy; 21. Lady Jane Fellowes; 22. Viscount Althorp; 23. Earl Spencer; 24. Mr Robert Fellowes; 25. Lady Sarah McCorquodale; 26. Mr. Neil McCorquodale.*

Above *At the Royal Variety Show, 1980, with Danny Kaye, Larry Hagman and Mary Martin.*

Opposite *Queen Elizabeth on a typical informal 'walkabout' – though during a day of high ceremonial in Dover: her installation as Lord Warden of the Cinque Ports on 1 August 1979.*

royal Sandringham estate. She and her sisters played and swam with two young princes named Andrew and Edward among neighbourhood groups of friends at holiday times.

The connection was not new. The Queen's family and the Spencers had lines of ancestry in common; and the Queen Mother, often at Sandringham, knew and liked the Spencer girls. Both the grandmothers of this future Princess of Wales – the late Countess Spencer and Lady Fermoy – were ladies-in-waiting to the Lady of Clarence House. (And could it have been, indeed, that the *Prince's* grandmother had been in some degree an architect of the romance?)

Diana's father, before he succeeded to the earldom and its stately home, Althorp near Northampton, was, as Viscount Althorp, an equerry to the present Queen in the first three years of her reign. And one of her sisters, Lady Jane, married Mr. Robert Fellowes, who is one of the Queen's Private Secretaries at Buckingham Palace.

Charles and Diana had come into adult consciousness of each other in 1977 at a pheasant shoot. (Diana was sixteen then.) At the 1981 betrothal-time the Prince recalled that he'd thought: 'What a very jolly, amusing and attractive girl.' His fiancée said she had found him 'pretty amazing'. The romance was something that flowered gradually; but as their meetings grew more and more frequent, sometimes at Balmoral and well away from the Press, interest grew to attraction and attraction grew to

love. So the couple's match was of their own choosing. There was no dynastic contriving and diplomatic arranging about it, as was almost always the case in the royal betrothals of past ages. When the betrothal photographs and interviews came, the pair were clearly in love. Which is what the public liked about it all. During that time of widespread excitement over the news, there was no such thing as reflecting on the age gap between the couple – it is thirteen years – or the inevitable differences in character and tastes: they would be 'good for each other'. That was, rightly, both their own view and the opinion of anyone who gave the point a thought. Only in later years was it noted that the Princess loved the bright lights of London as the Prince loved the bare heights of Lochnagar. But nothing wrong in that either. (The Press cameras have worked overtime on presenting visions of the Princess of Wales and those bright lights, the Diana of the pop-music concerts; whereas, for instance, her days of quiet work on committees of children's charities go completely unreported – as she wishes.)

In early 1981, when she sprang into foremost news, the journalists scrambled to dig out every possible detail about a girl so recently unknown. Lady Diana Spencer, they found, was the third and youngest daughter of the eighth Earl Spencer and his first wife, formerly the Honourable Frances Roche, and now, on her second marriage (which ended in 1988), Mrs. Shand-Kydd, whose husband had farming and business interests in Scotland and in Australia. Diana's parents had separated when she was six. Her father married again, and the present Countess Spencer is Raine, formerly Lady Dartmouth, daughter of the writer of romantic fiction, Barbara Cartland.

In her schooldays, Diana was undistinguished in classroom and in playing-fields, but became a school senior, and a liked one, by her character: she was self-reliant, cheerful and good-tempered – and adored pet animals, babies, and small children.

Opposite, top *'She's all right!'* This picture brought universal sighs of relief. The Queen Mother emerges from hospital in December 1982 after an emergency operation for the removal of a fish-bone from her throat which had been choking her – and caused world alarm.

Left *Grandeur of setting and assembled guests beneath the dome of St. Paul's – another Eightieth Birthday picture, showing the Queen Mother, the Queen and Prince Philip at the front of the congregation. The City sword lies before the Sovereign.*

Opposite, bottom *August 4, 1982, was a date of double celebration. It was the Queen Mother's Eighty-second birthday and was chosen as the day of the Christening of her great-grandson, Prince William, then little more than six weeks old. The ceremony took place at the Palace, where this picture of four generations was taken. The infant Second-in-Line was comforted only by sucking the little finger of his mother, the Princess of Wales.*

Her headmistress said she was 'marvellous with people'. So it was hardly surprising that in her late teens she had taken to teaching at a kindergarten in Pimlico, London. The school, and the flat which Diana shared with two other girls, was under media siege day and night during the weeks before her engagement to the Prince was announced officially. It was difficult for her to have a moment's peace or privacy, but she behaved with remarkable aplomb under the photographers' flash-bulbs and the journalists' questions.

The game of battling her own way through phalanxes of pressmen ended as soon as the betrothal secret was out. Lady Diana Spencer then came under the protective umbrella of the Royal Family. It was impossible to live any longer with her flatmates. She had to dive for cover and operate from a new base. So where did she go to live in the run-up to the wedding? Where else but the home of her fiancé's Golden Grannie, Clarence House.

July 29 was fixed as the marriage date, and St. Paul's Cathedral – not the traditional Abbey – was Prince Charles's choice for the ceremony. And when the Wedding Day came it proved to be, beyond wildest dreams, perfect picture-book stuff. A summer of miserable weather suddenly produced hours of sunshine to match the glow of the proceedings. It was all very human and very handsome. Personal tenderness at the altar, and a family's genuine happiness touched the emotions of all who were witnesses. There was a catch now and then even in the throats of professed republican cynics and blasé professional observers. Never had there been such a mammoth media event. It was watched by a million people on the London streets and,

Fashion-plate Lady meets a rock fan of the Eighties dressed in heavy-metal fashion. Her Majesty, in July, 1982, was visiting young people on adventure training courses at St. Katharine's Dock. The youth had strapped on all his studded leather gear for the occasion.

'live' on television, by 800-million viewers from Yokohama to the Yukon. And was a joy, a pleasure to see. Not just a show for tourists, not just an Establishment extravaganza; but a People's Day.

Also, a long and hard-working day for a great many people concerned with the event. Nowhere was busier than the Queen Mother's home, the place from which the bride of the Prince of Wales set out for her wedding. Diana had stayed overnight at Clarence House, which was a keypoint in the whole Operation Marriage. Things were buzzing there before 6 a.m. Arrivals at Queen Elizabeth's household-door were headed by the bouquet florists, the hairdresser, the make-up girl, a ladies' maid, a lady-in-waiting from the Palace, and the designers of Lady Diana's gown, the young Welsh couple, Elizabeth and David Emanuel. The dressing of the young bride in their creation, yards and yards of crushed ivory silk taffeta, topped by a tiara-crowned floating veil and a white train twenty-five feet long – all that took so long that the wearer of that 'fashion sensation' had hardly any time to pause and sit down until she was in the Glass Coach and away to the Cathedral with her father beside her.

The Queen Mother herself – who also had been up very early

to greet the assembling family, friends, bridesmaids and pages – was a striking enough picture in a gown of aquamarine silk. In all the day's pageantry of processions she was the first of the principal figures to drive out from the house, to St. Paul's through the miles of cheering people, taking grandson Prince Edward with her. (The young prince, seventeen then, and taking part in his first royal procession, was a 'supporter' of his bridegroom brother at the marriage service. There is no 'best man' at a royal wedding such as this, but two supporters – Prince Andrew was the other one: he drove to St. Paul's with Prince Charles, and had the honour of riding with the Queen Mother in the procession back from cathedral to Buckingham Palace.)

Highlights of the marriage service remain in the memory. The full-dress magnificence and variety of the congregation, for instance, including Crowned Heads from overseas, our own Royal Family in all its branches, famous statesmen, *plus* many of the bridegroom's personal friends, stars of the variety stage and stand-up comics among them. A pretty sight was Lady Sarah Armstrong-Jones (Princess Margaret's daughter, then aged seventeen) acting as train bearer and leading Lady Diana's attendants: young children frisking along as bridesmaids and pages. The children were an assortment indeed: among them were a pupil from the school where the bride had taught, a daughter of Prince Charles's racehorse trainer, a great-granddaughter of Sir Winston Churchill, and eleven-year-old Lord Nicholas Windsor, youngest child of the Duke and Duchess of Kent's family.

The music in St. Paul's was a rare feast: Purcell, Bach, Holst, Walton, and of course thundering Elgar. There were great fanfares of trumpets and a splendid massing of singers and orchestras. During the signing of the marriage register, the New Zealand opera star, Miss Kiri Te Kanawa, with the Bach Choir, sang the 'Let the bright Seraphim' aria from Handel's *Samson*. All the cathedral sounds, and every word spoken, were relayed outside through loud-speakers hung along the streets; and many people in the crowds joined in the singing and the prayers.

Both in the return processions and on the Palace balcony afterwards, the Queen Mother drew notably fervent cheers, but of course the bride and groom were the centrepieces of the numerous balcony appearances – during which there came an instantly-famous highpoint of informality, perhaps best described by a cockney in the crowd below as 'a proper big smacker of a kiss between Charlie and his girl – no one's ever seen Royals do such a thing in public before'.

Such was that summer day in 1981 when the Royal Family acquired an attractive new member, who was to become in the following years the most photographed female in the land. Unceasingly, the twenty-first English Princess of Wales was rich media forage. Her popularity, certainly the interest in her, have shown no sign of decline, however many rival Press targets came into view. At the same time, inevitably, as she developed from a shy twenty-year-old bride to an assured wife and loving mother – and fashion plate – there were stories of high-hat bossiness as well as healthy high spirits, of nervous loneliness and insecurity at first as well as warm confidence in public engagements. In these, Diana has shown herself to be both diligent and sincerely caring.

From the start, she got on well with the family, the House of Windsor to which she had brought new brightness 'from the outside' just as Elizabeth Bowes-Lyon had done sixty years and two generations before.

Before 1981 was out, and honeymoon still bright in the

Above *Princess Michael of Kent and her husband (left) join the race-going scene and regular occupants of the Royal Box at Epsom. A picture on Derby Day, 1980.*

Below *An impulsive cockney salute from a meat porter to London's 'Queen Mum' on tour in Smithfield Market, 1982.*

memory, came official word that the Princess was expecting a child – and the Queen Mother looked forward to being a great-grandmother for the third time.

The baby was born on the longest day of the summer of 1982: June 21. (Perhaps it seemed, to him, to be the *father's* longest day too: the Prince of Wales went to St. Mary's Hospital, Paddington, with his wife and stayed at the hospital at the Princess's side for sixteen hours, until the baby's birth.) It was a boy! The glad news was flashed round the world – but not until a delighted grandson had made a swift 'phone call to Queen Elizabeth at Clarence House; and of course another to the Palace. *This* great-grandson – to be named William of Wales and a Prince from the start – was of paramount importance, not to be superseded in the Succession: Second-in-Line to the Throne.

All was well at the birth, so much so that on the very next day the Princess walked out of the hospital, bright and smiling, taking turns with the proud father at cradling and holding up the seven-pound infant for all the world to see. From the five minutes of exhibiting on the hospital steps the parents drove William off to the nursery at their new London home, a set of apartments in Kensington Palace.

The baptism of the lively William Arthur Philip Louis came several weeks later, felicitously timed in fact as an extra salute for the Queen Mother's birthday on August 4 that year, when she became 82 years of age. So, after beaming radiantly on the singing and cheering crowds at her own gates, Queen Elizabeth drove along the Mall to Buckingham Palace, where the baptismal service took place in the handsome Music Room which has often served as a chapel for royal christenings since World War Two. The baby behaved impeccably during the half-hour service, but it was a different story at the long photo-call for group pictures afterwards. William, lovely though he looked in the famous lace christening robe handed down from Queen Victoria's days, was hungry and bored and bothered by the bright lamps of the cameramen, and soon was howling inconsolably as he was held in turn by grandmother and great-grandmother. His noise did not stop until his mother took him in her arms and popped her little finger into his mouth. At which the child sucked the digit with mighty gusto and manifest hope.

The Queen Mother had regarded her tiny descendant's hullabaloo with equanimity. 'Quite right,' she said. 'He's wanting lunch; he's made his first public speech; and he's got good lungs.' It was at any rate a significant start. Unlike his father – Charles was a shy and thoughtful little boy – this roaring royal child has continued to be a boisterous extrovert, a regular 'handful', during the years which have been turning him from babyhood to boyhood. Indeed, even when he was only two years old he did his best to be an energetic 'minder' of his new baby brother Prince Harry, who was born on September 15, 1984, and christened Henry Charles Albert David.

But in 1982, before the birth of William, it was a somewhat older and undoubtedly a most ebullient member of the Royal Family who was in the headlines. Prince Andrew, aged 22 then, the husky uncle of the Wales boys, serving in the Royal Navy as a Fleet Air Arm helicopter pilot, was in action and in considerable personal hazard during the gravest international event of that year: the costly campaign to liberate the Falkland Islands from Argentinian invasion. Andrew was in the thick of the fighting.

Afterwards, his grandmother Queen Elizabeth made a point of welcoming home some of the heroes of those South Atlantic

A Prince in the South Atlantic War, 1982. Sub-Lieutenant Prince Andrew, then a navy helicopter pilot in the Falklands campaign, steps ashore with a fellow crewman from their ship, HMS Invincible. *The battle for Port Stanley had just been won.*

battles of May and June. It was on a day when she, as Lord Warden of the Cinque Ports, was visiting Britain's south coast harbours on board the Royal Yacht. Sailing from Dover to Portsmouth, she diverted the *Britannia* to make rendezvous in the West Solent with the liner *Queen Elizabeth II* which had been converted to be a troopship and was bringing back survivors of naval vessels sunk in the Falklands engagements. Thus the occasion was a salute from a real Queen to a famous ocean 'Queen'; and as the trooper passed the Yacht men crowded her rails to see Her Majesty waving from the deck of the royal ship. Signals were exchanged, and the cheering to *her* echoed loudly across the water.

Lieutenant Prince Andrew himself enjoyed a festive return when his ship, H.M.S. *Invincible*, came back home and had an exuberant reception from families headed by his own relatives.

The Royal Family experienced its own alarms and excursions during 1982, in different and domestic ways. At Royal Lodge, Windsor, one evening after dinner, Queen Elizabeth got a fishbone lodged intractably in her throat, and, local medical efforts failing, had to be rushed to a London hospital in the middle of the night. Next morning the world was made fearful by newspaper headlines crying 'Queen Mother – an Emergency Operation'. It was not an exaggeration. A general anaesthetic

In tour after tour, Canada has long been a favourite country for Queen Elizabeth, who has visited every Province. Here she has just landed at an airfield near Halifax, Nova Scotia to present Maritime Command colours; but, characteristically, she first had to chat with waiting children.

had to be administered before the bone could be extracted. But, after hours during which anxiety had throbbed through the world's news networks, the medical signal was: 'All's well.' There had been no panic on the patient's part. To everyone's relief, and astonishment too, Her Majesty, smiling and brightly dressed in familiar style, walked out of the hospital door after a stay of only one night. 'The fish had fought back,' she said.

Palace Intruder

The most dangerous royal happening of the year was something beyond the wildest imagining, and was deep inside Buckingham Palace itself. One morning in mid-July Queen Elizabeth the Second, 'safe' in her own home, woke to find an intruder in her bedroom – a dishevelled, barefooted man, talking incoherently and trying to draw the curtains. The startling stranger, it turned out, had been able to arrive on this of all scenes because of incredible flaws in constabulary duties and mechanical devices at the headquarters of the monarchy: in short, security had failed or had been easily overcome. The man, having surmounted walls and windows, had been wandering round numerous Palace rooms unchallenged, and was now sitting on the Monarch's bed waving a broken ashtray in a bloodstained hand.

Hard to believe though this was, and is, the Queen – who kept marvellously calm – was unguarded: no one was at that moment outside her room, the duty footman was taking the corgis for a walk in the garden, and it was several minutes before the Palace police made any appearance despite the Queen's repeated telephone and alarm-bell calls to their duty room. It was the Sovereign herself, and a suddenly emerging maidservant, who kept the raider at bay – in fact, conducted him to, and detained him in, a nearby pantry by sheer talking to him until help came.

Since that time, the setting up of a special Royal Protection squad has fundamentally altered the circumstances in which royal premises and persons are safeguarded.

But that startling incident of 1982 must have recalled suddenly and vividly to the Queen *Mother's* mind an experience which was thrust upon *her* forty years before (it is a memory which suggests that the present Queen has inherited her mother's remarkable self-control and composure). The drama then was during the Second World War when Her Majesty was Queen Consort and was staying overnight at Windsor Castle. She was in her room, about to finish dressing to go down to dinner, when a deserter from the Army, who had been masquerading as a civilian workman, having gained access to the room earlier, leapt out from behind a curtain. He grabbed the Queen by the ankles, stammering out a story about wanting royal help because he had lost all his family in an air raid and was desperate about the whole war situation. He looked upset to the point of madness; and the Queen, thinking that here was someone in a dangerous emotional state and who would probably have harmed her if she had screamed, stood stock still and said: 'Just tell me about it.' The intruder let go his hold and the Queen walked slowly towards a wall where she could press a bell. Having done that, she kept the stowaway talking until help came and he was led away. 'I was sorry for him,' she said later. 'He really meant no harm after all.'

Probably the Queen Mother has never panicked about anything at all, certainly never about her own safety. She worries about other people, but usually is quite cavalier over her own welfare and health. Her activities continued to be most strongly pursued through all the unfolding of the very eventful and at times frightening Eighties. No slowing-down, no dodging of commitments, and no reduction in the number of her engagements and travels.

Memory has been a friend and sustainer to her through the later years. She has even cherished memorial services because of their reminders of contemporaries who gave her joy in their lifetimes. One thinks of the Westminster Abbey service in March 1984 at which her friend Noël Coward was gratefully and musically remembered. Her Majesty was guest of honour; she

laid a remembrance stone, and took part in the singing of several of the enduring Coward numbers which made that whole ceremony an occasion charged with nostalgia to the last note of 'I'll see you again'.

She has shone at innumerable theatre gatherings, and stage people love her. When she attends the great charity event, the Royal Variety Performance, she herself, as she sits in the royal box, is the star of the evening. There is a rule that performers may bow to the box but must *play* to the audience. But there was one night at the Palladium when one man broke the rule. It was the late Maurice Chevalier, who, at the end of his marvellous fifteen-minute turn, brought the house down by swinging left, going down on one knee, and singing directly to the Queen Mother the song which begins 'You must have been a beautiful baby', to which he improvised a final line:"Cos, Majesty, look at you now!' The entire audience rose to its feet and gave an ovation the like of which has rarely been heard.

To return to the story of the recent years, 1984 has to be picked out again if only to recall that one of Queen Elizabeth's happiest of many Continental travels marked the autumn of that year. For a few days she revelled in the art and the ardour of Northern Italy; taking the Royal Yacht *Britannia* up the Adriatic, she toured Venice, and enchanted the whole region. On a canal trip by gondola, she was appropriately accompanied by the Flag Officer Royal Yachts!

Two years later, another trip to Italy, a private visit this time, but a particular personal joy. She was not an official person: she was a tourist, a tourist remembering a very distant past when she, a little girl called Elizabeth Bowes-Lyon, went to Tuscany. For one of the places she went to during the springtime visit to Florence was an old mansion on a hillside looking out over the

Tuscan capital: the Villa Capponi, set in enchanting grounds, and last seen by this royal visitor 75 years before. It was then the home of Elizabeth's maternal grandmother, no less – she who had become Mrs. Scott by a second marriage after the death of her Cavendish-Bentinck first husband. There is little doubt that the Queen Mother's knowledge of flowers and trees and shrubs, and her love of the sunny outdoors and cultivated hillsides, has come down to her from childhood and from that ancestor who went to live in a Florentine villa two generations before Queen Elizabeth's own. For Mrs. Scott's talents and skills as a gardener were famous, and not only round her Italian home.

Queen Elizabeth is rarely without masses of flowers about her. Even so, the birthday anniversaries sometimes bring more than she can manage. That was particularly true of August the Fourth 1985, an exceptional occasion because for once Her Majesty spent the day, a Sunday, at Sandringham instead of London. It proved to be a shocking wet day; and when in very heavy rain she and her daughters emerged from the Sandringham estate's little Church of St. Mary Magdalene after morning service the Queen Mother was almost inundated by gifts from a crowd of six thousand people who had waited outside in the downpour. Scores of children rushed forward pressing their tributes on her. For several minutes, her umbrella unopened, she stood talking to the frontline boys and girls and receiving masses of flowers and cards – far too many to hold. 'Help, please, everybody,' she said, beckoning to her family and house guests standing near. She then organized a not-unwilling 'chain gang' and began passing along, from hand to hand, bunches of roses, carnations and sweet peas. First, the floral tide flowed to the Queen, then Princess Margaret, then to the Prince of Wales, then the ladies-in-waiting, and so on to the hands of secretaries, detectives and policewomen so that at the end of the

Opposite *'Monty' is ten feet tall as Queen Elizabeth in Whitehall unveils the statue of Field Marshall Viscount Montgomery of Alamein. This was June 6, 1980, thirty-six years after the D-day landings of World War Two.*

Right *In his mother's arms and only one day old (this was June 22, 1982), baby Prince William of Wales emerges from the Paddington hospital where he was born, to be driven home to Kensington Palace.*

line all the blooms could be placed in a brilliant mass beside the path ready to be taken up to the Big House.

Everybody was 'in the act' – and in the news pictures.

Going to church on that special day was not just a routine bit of Birthday Programme. It could never have been merely a required parade. She had been at private Holy Communion very early that morning in front of the Sandringham church's silver altar. Had she been in London, as so often on her birthday, the Queen Mother, unreported, would have taken communion in the quiet of the Chapel Royal within St. James's Palace.

Religious acts, yes; worship in church has been part of all Her Majesty's years. Her life is sustained by a Christian faith and belief which is deep and personal. Her practices have always been firmly based on – in her own words – 'moral truths which do not alter with a changing world'. Her religion transcends sectarian divisions. And, wherever she is, there is nothing dour or dull or automatic about her own morality and any manifestations of it.

In any case, during every year many of Queen Elizabeth's diary engagements take her into churches, as might be expected. Some events are solemn rituals to which duty demands attendance; but certain of the services stay in the memory specially as occasions of family enjoyment in thanksgiving. Such was the gathering in St. George's Chapel at Windsor Castle on April 21, 1986, to mark the sixtieth birthday of her daughter, the Queen. That celebration was one of the year's highlights.

But only eight days later the Royal Family were in that chapel again – this time a sombre assembly. They were there for the funeral of the Duchess of Windsor who had died on April 24, at 90, having outlived her husband by 14 years. For almost a decade she had been a sick woman, lying in a darkened room in her Paris house. Long past were the days when she was bright Bessie Warfield Simpson from America, and then the famous divorcée whose attraction for Edward VIII brought about the 1936 Abdication which was such a disruptive influence on the British Crown and so dramatic a turning point in the life of Elizabeth Bowes-Lyon. Now, at the end of Wallis's long sad story, that Duchess – never accorded the style of a Highness – was royally honoured in death as she had not been in life: a full family funeral ceremony at the Castle, after which she was laid to rest beside her husband at the burial ground of kings within Windsor's Frogmore Gardens. It was April 29, a melancholy day.

Andrew of York

But the principal event of 1986 was a happy one. This was another wedding year. The high point of its summer was the marriage of the robust, attractively spirited second-son of the Sovereign, Prince Andrew. Historians of the future will log the pageantry of it all, but may slim their record of the day by putting Andrew's nuptials down as simply 'a joyous repeat of the

wedding of Prince Charles five years before.' (They may also note that both brides were from 'broken homes'.) It is true that the two marriage celebrations were similar, and the publicizing of the 1986 ceremonial was almost on the same vast scale as that of the Heir to the Throne; but the spontaneous shine of the Prince Andrew romance, and the public pleasure it gave, merits a special place in the Windsor Story. And the natural glow, the personal delight, which the bride radiated will be remembered for a long time. She was high spirits personified.

Just as today's Queen Mother, as a young woman over sixty years ago, brought infectious breeziness and sparkling humanity into the Palace compounds, so Andrew's Sarah, in 1986, noticeably refreshed 'the Royals' once again as she entered the Family Firm from a vigorous world outside. In this case, the lady brought rampageousness too!

The engagement was announced in March. The ebullient Andrew, aged 26, a lieutenant in the Royal Navy – and a young man who had been given (before the hard testing of the Falklands war) a reputation as a carefree playboy, frisky escort of pretty girls – was to marry a lively, titian-haired firework of a Modern Miss as assured, experienced and uncomplicated as himself. His chosen lady was Miss Sarah Ferguson, also 26, daughter of cavalry Major Ronald Ferguson (of the Life Guards, and Prince Charles's polo manager) and Mrs. Hector Barrantes (who parted with her family and country when daughter Sarah was in her early teens and made a second marriage to an Argentinian polo player – after which the galloping major married again; and Sarah was known to 'get on famously' with her stepmother and the young children of that marriage).

Sarah had been spotted as 'Andrew's likely one' by the Press-photography troops several weeks before the official announce-

*Here the Queen Mother is at Westminster Abbey to present a special
Children of Courage award to thirteen handicapped youngsters. The
girl on the left was blind, yet swam, rode and cycled. She could not see
the royal smile but would not forget the Visitor's voice and glow of
personality.*

Scotland, had come ashore from the Royal Yacht to spend a few hours with Grannie.

Finding that the Queen Mother was having difficulty in swallowing, it was decided that more than local attention was needed. On signals from the Queen herself to her Air Force, Queen Elizabeth was airlifted out of Mey by helicopter straight to hospital in Aberdeen for tests on the spasms of throat constriction. The patient allowed herself to be detained in Aberdeen overnight, but next day, quite better, she 'choppered' cheerfully back to her Caithness home to resume the brief holiday there.

In that same year, during the long autumn sojourn at Birkhall on royal Deeside – the happy weeks which as usual followed the Mey time – Queen Elizabeth had a fall whilst out walking, and suffered a small cut on a leg. Nothing was confessed about this until her return to London in November. It seemed then that the injury was not satisfactorily healing, and five days of observation and treatment in hospital ensued. Public anxiety erupted at once.

Large newspaper headings saying 'Queen Mother Enters Hospital' were more symptoms of concern than scaremongering. This was the lady the country could not do without, the 'Royal' who (for 50 years a Queen) had always been reassuringly part of the nation's life. But people need not have worried. She was back on duty within a week, out-sparkling her own tiara with her smile as she arrived at the Theatre Royal, Drury Lane, for the Royal Variety Performance, and, to general delight, with a dazzling young Duchess of York in tow – glamorous grannie and national newlywed, two generations apart but starring together.

Class of '87

The younger generation were in the headlines frequently during the next year, 1987. It was early in the January that the student prince, Edward, made his jarring decision to resign from the Royal Marines. A hard thing to do, against tradition and the wishes of his father (Prince Philip is Captain General of the Marines), but Prince Edward was firm in mind and took this unexpected step not long after coming down from Cambridge at the age of 22. The Prince evidently felt that, although he had not failed to make the grade in the Corps' tough commando training, the military life was not, after all, for him. To continue would have been an unfulfilling pretence, something against his nature and his heart. So, painfully, he left a destined course, and seemed in a limbo. Little more than a year later he was to take another unprecedented step by entering into a regular paid job – off-stage and at a learner's level – in the commerical theatre, becoming a production assistant ('willing dogsbody', an associate put it) in Andrew Lloyd Webber's firm. He did indeed start at the bottom, in London, tea-making and doing paperwork at the company's Palace Theatre office. Edward had noticeably enjoyed unversity student theatricals; but this was different, an attempt to be – his own words were: 'exactly the same as everybody else' – whilst one of a team of enthusiastic stage production workers. It would not always be easy. There remained the matter of security, Royal Protection, for one thing. No one so close to the Throne had ever embarked on a civilian professional career – and certainly not in the theatre.

This prince did continue to carry out public engagements, however, undertaking social work as well, especially when it was concerned with raising Good Cause money. As time went on he managed to tackle many royal engagements, especially for the Duke of Edinburgh's Award schemes, as well as his theatre activities.

Several times in busy 1987 he helped charity events. He was the leader of what was called The Grand Knockout Tournament, a sponsored and televised programme of silly games in fancy dress. It was played in a country house garden by teams of show-business and sporting characters divided into four teams captained by Princess Anne, the Duke and Duchess of York, and Edward himself, whose idea it was. The performances of competitive buffoonery went on for a long time, and everybody was either in medieval rig or costumed as cartoon figures, animals, or animated vegetables. The captains did not themselves perform knockabout turns or crawl through drainpipes, but cheered the frantic foolery. Prince Edward had declared: 'There's too much seriousness in the world: people should sometimes let their hair down and have fun.' However, the antics had a mixed reception, numerous viewers feeling that they dented respect for royalty and royal usefulness.

Queen Elizabeth, *in absentia*, perhaps raised an eyebrow at this particular manifestation of frolicking new-style royalty, but probably smiled as she switched-off. Narrow-minded disapproval does not come naturally to her, and she has never expected the young ones to conform to every old pattern. It is *their* world.

She herself is not hide-bound and not always predictable. She spontaneously made a change in the Birthday Appearance of 1987. When she walked out of the Clarence House gates on *that* August day to thank the waiting crowds and gather armfuls of flowers and greeting cards, with members of the family watching, two paces back, she went strolling forward instead of the customary farewell wave and retreat into the garden. To the surprise of her detective, secretary, butler, daughters and attendant corgis, she made a sortie along the street, surrounded by people and accepting more posies and presents at every step. The old magic was still there: everybody went home thinking they had been personally thanked and specially smiled at. As indeed they had.

Then it was off to Scotland as usual, to her homes at Mey and Birkhall to spend the latter part of summer and the autumn. This time the annual break had scarcely begun when there was sudden and melancholy news from another part of her Scotland, from Glamis, the home of Her Majesty's very early years. Her visits to the Castle had become rare, but now a message from there made a journey to the old house imperative, and a sad return it was. Two weeks after her birthday, her nephew Fergus, seventeenth Earl of Strathmore, head of the Bowes-Lyon family, collapsed and died on the moors of his Scottish estate. His funeral, a private one held in the Chapel at the Castle, was attended by the Queen and Prince Philip and Princess Margaret as well as the Queen Mother. This Lord Strathmore, who was 58, had spent comparatively little time at the family home in recent years (he kept a residence in Spain, where he had business enterprises), and it was his wife Mary, the Countess, who had been for the most part in charge at the castle and keenly identified with the big development her husband had started: the building up of Glamis as a regular tourist attraction. Her son Michael, Lord Glamis, is now the eighteenth Earl. His father's death brought him an early succession to the title, for he was only thirty – 57 years younger than the most famous of the living Bowes-Lyons, his royal great-aunt, the world's 'Queen Mum'.

Above *Uniquely waterborne, the royal lady (in the autumn of 1984) went sightseeing along a canal in Venice. In the gondola, she was escorted by H.M.Y. Britannia's admiral – Flag Officer Royal Yachts!*

Left *April 29, 1986, a day of mourning and memories of sad years past: Her Majesty in St. George's Chapel, Windsor Castle, for the funeral service and burial of the Duchess of Windsor.*

Opposite *August 1, 1979. As the new Lord Warden and Admiral of the Cinque Ports, Her Majesty drives down from Dover Castle, whose Constable she also has just become.*

But it is not the Queen Mother's own way to measure generation gaps. Or to slow down either. Another thing which the year 1987 showed was her unwillingness to eliminate overseas dates from her engagement diary. She flew across the Atlantic to Canada yet again that summer (a twelfth visit to the old and favourite dominion), and this time it was to be present at the celebrations in Montreal of the hundred-and-twenty-fifth anniversary of the Black Watch of Canada, of which Highland Regiment she has been Colonel-in-Chief ever since she was crowned Queen Consort. She has of course been 'mother of the regiment' of Scotland's own Black Watch since that time too.

This time in Canada there were three days only, and officially

Above *It was as a newly-ducal Prince Andrew and Miss Sarah Ferguson that the present Duke and Duchess of York went to the altar in Westminster Abbey on a sparkling July 23, 1986. (Note the small pages and bridesmaids – front row, left.)*

Opposite *Nobody, it seemed, enjoyed that Royal Wedding of 1986 more than the exuberant couple themselves. Here Their Royal Highnesses, man and wife, popularly called 'Andrew and Fergie', pass the Family on starting the walk down the aisle.*

Right *Prince William of Wales was unabashed – even in 1987 when he was only five – by the cameras and the throngs as he travelled with his great-grannie and his mother to the Trooping the Colour parade.*

Below *The kiss that brought a crescendo of cheers from the wedding-day crowds below the Palace balcony after the Abbey ceremony. Informal as always, the Yorks had no inhibitions about answering the shouts of 'let's see a proper smacker!'*

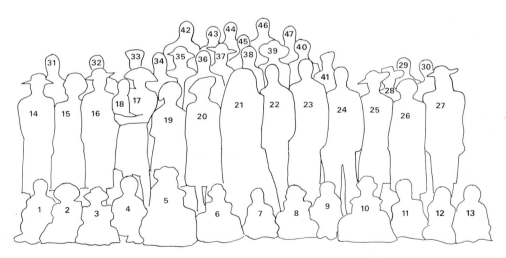

1986. The full group for the Family Album. The Royal Wedding group. FRONT ROW, SEATED, LEFT TO RIGHT: *1, The Earl of Ulster; 2, Lady Davina Windsor; 3, Lady Rose Windsor; 4, Andrew Ferguson; 5, Lady Rosanagh Innes-Ker; 6, Zara Phillips; 7, Prince William; 8, Laura Fellowes; 9, Seamus Makim; 10, Alice Ferguson; 11, Peter Phillips; 12, Lady Gabriella Windsor; 13, Lord Frederick Windsor.* SECOND ROW: *14, Lady Sarah Armstrong-Jones; 15, Princess Margaret; 16, Princess Anne; 17, Princess Diana holding Prince Henry 18; 19, the Queen Mother; 20, the Queen; 21, the Duchess of York; 22, the Duke of York; 23, Major Ronald Ferguson; 24, Prince*

Edward; 25, Mrs Hector Barrantes; 26, Lady Elmhirst; 27, Mrs Jane Makim. SLIGHTLY BEHIND THEM: *28, the Hon Mrs Doreen Wright; 29, Major Bryan Wright; 30, Alexander Makim.* THIRD ROW: *31, Viscount Linley; 32, Captain Mark Phillips; 33. Marina Ogilvy; 34, Prince Charles; 35, Princess Alexandra; 36, the Duke of Edinburgh; 37, Princess Michael of Kent; 38, Princess Alice; 39, the Duchess of Gloucester; 40, the Duchess of Kent; 41, Lady Helen Windsor.* BACK ROW: *42, James Ogilvy; 43, Prince Michael of Kent; 44, the Hon Angus Ogilvy; 45, the Duke of Gloucester; 46, the Duke of Kent; 47, the Earl of St. Andrews.*

179

Above *The Lady of Clarence House is no mere cocktails-in-salons Queen. She likes to get out and 'meet the real people'. Here, she has broken away from an official tour in London's east-end to pop into a Stepney pub. Offered champagne, she declined and opted for a glass of bitter.*

Opposite, top *Each December brings a visit to the Smithfield Show at the famous market in the City of London. Her Majesty has been a prizewinner too, with an Aberdeen Angus heifer from her herd of cattle at the Castle of Mey.*

Opposite, bottom *This little girl, aged 9, couldn't wait another four days to go to London to give flowers to her 'Queen Mum' on the exact eighty-eighth birthday anniversary. So on Sunday, 31 July, she waited outside Sandringham Church with a special posy for Her Majesty as she came out after attending morning service.*

it was simply a military occasion. But, predictably, the host country did not leave it at that. She had come to salute certain soldiers, all well and good, but Canada seized another opportunity to salute *her*; and the programme eventually bulged with a series of welcomes staged by the Canadian Government, the whole French-speaking Province of Quebec, and the great city and port of Montreal itself.

The visit proved to be a 72-hour marathon of engagements which – so it seemed to those who watched – would have taxed the stamina of a young Olympic athlete. But the octogenarian lady who was centre of it all sailed through the schedule with no apparent strain, enjoying everything from her first speech – slipping easily into her fluent French – to the last regimental swing of parading kilts across the stadium and the last shrilling skirl of the pipes across the waters of the St. Lawrence. It was three days in a modern, self-governing Canada which had cut all

Opposite, top *A proud father gets into one of the early pictures. The Duke and Duchess of York share a safe hold on their firstborn child.*

Opposite, bottom *The photograph taken by Prince Andrew (though he, the Duke of York, is in the picture) immediately after the christening of Princess Beatrice in the Chapel Royal of St. James's Palace in London, five days before the Family's Sandringham Christmas of 1988.*
  This official group includes H.M. The Queen, The Queen Mother, others of the immediate family, and the baby's five godparents.

Above *Splendour of dress, Western and Eastern, is seen as the Queen Mother joins the Queen and Prince Philip in a Buckingham Palace welcome to King Fahd of Saudi Arabia. A pre-banquet group during the king's State Visit in 1987.*

Right *A regular March engagement for Queen Elizabeth is her St. Patrick's Day distribution of shamrock to the Irish Guards. The regimental mascot gets a share, here at Chelsea Barracks.*

colonial links with Britain; it was three days in a Province of separatist leanings. But there was no evidence of any such background. It was – because the visitor was the Queen Mother – a three-day exhibition of enthusiasm for the old Royal Connection.

Soon after she had flown home to London, Her Majesty was off again, this time to the linked anniversary date – in Berlin. For 'her own' soldiers, the first battalion the Black Watch, were stationed at the Montgomery Barracks there, and her inspection was a special marking of her fiftieth year as the regiment's Colonel-in-Chief.

Then it was straight back to busy weeks in Britain, her autumn diary full of appointments right up to the Family Christmas, and then into 1988. Working on and on; and planning for her Nineties. There was no resting on laurels – no need and no wish for that.

The new year of 1989 found Her Majesty full of zest, sustained by her own activity and the regard of everyone around her.

At the time of writing this further edition of a long life story, I can add that new years and also new generations of the busy royal family are bringing changes in the 'firm's' public performance and style, so that the whole atmosphere surrounding the House of Windsor has in some areas altered immensely. The 'Palace world' is different indeed from the shuttered society which Elizabeth Bowes-Lyon breezed into well over half a century ago. Her descendants are under unrelenting media scrutiny and criticism – which they have come to expect and to live with. But a general press as well as public opinion is that Britain's 'family monarchy' is still worthwhile and wanted. And the lady of Clarence House has a good deal of responsibility for that.

To her, and to the country, recent times, inevitably, have brought losses and sorrows as well as joyful experiences. There were the air and rail crashes of 1988 and 1989, and the shocking football crowd disaster in Sheffield.

A personal calamity, in the March of '88, struck at the heart of the Royal House. That was when an avalanche caught the Prince of Wales's skiing party who had gone out on a dangerous slope at the Swiss resort of Klosters and killed one of Prince Charles's companions, Major Hugh Lindsay, a former equerry at the Palace and friend of the family. The Prince himself narrowly escaped death; and Queen Elizabeth shared her grandson's lingering distress over the tragedy.

Brighter happenings came later, especially during the ensuing August when Sarah, the new Duchess of York, gave birth to her first child, a daughter, the Queen Mother's fifth great-grandchild. The infant Princess was given the first name of Beatrice, a name which means 'bringer of joy'. And certainly joyful did the parents, Prince Andrew and his wife, seem as, with care and pride, they held the baby up for the official photographs. Father Andrew, a skilled photographer himself, snapped picture after picture.

Not surprisingly, however, the most publicly manifest excitement over the new arrival had begun several days before the actual birth (which came on a date said to be very auspicious: 8.8.88) as, night after night, television audiences saw the massed ranks of camera-toting newsmen camped and waiting in the street outside the London private hospital to which the Duchess had gone. Inordinate press coverage of the birth was of course a measure of the persistent public interest in the high-spirited 'Fergie'. But by the time the day came when

mother and daughter at last emerged from the hospital door, many viewers as well as the crews of physically wearied journalistic vigilantes confessed that they had really 'had enough'. It was not, however, the first or the last 'media overkill' of the year.

By contrast, the scenes and sentiments attending the Queen Mother's birthday anniversaries seemed to go on purveying unalloyed enjoyment to pressmen, to television viewers, and to the hundreds of people spontaneously cheering outside the gates of Clarence House. The informal Birthday Walkabouts from those gates have so long had an established pattern that every thread of variant is always well reported – and accepted as 'great fun' by Queen Elizabeth herself. For instance, there was her patient pause for several minutes in one stroll up the street called Stable Yard to enable a man in the crowd to read to her face three verses of a Happy Anniversary poem which he had composed for the occasion.

One of the remembered excursions of Summer 1988 was in the few hours Her Majesty spent by making a scheduled visit to the Surrey side of the lower Thames. On the face of it, her engagement was not a very exciting one: she had been invited to view building developments in the regenerated Docklands area. But, thanks to the Visitor's natural flair for putting life and laughter into the bare bones of a primly planned programme, the event produced an unconventional hour or two of chatting with East-Enders who crowded the streets of her route because they remembered, as she did, the wartime visits of King and Queen to the still-smoking ruins of blitz-bombed streets down there.

Embracing the atmosphere of the Cockney afternoon, Her Majesty (to give one example of the fun that went on) stopped her car outside a well-favoured pub in the Rotherhithe-Stepney area and marched inside – to the delight of the landlord and his friends and customers of course. She was at once offered a glass of champagne; but no, she declined that with a smile and ordered a pint of bitter in the saloon bar. It wasn't 'putting on an act', it was natural: 'the Queen Mum touch'.

Looking at the numbers and pace of royal public engagements nowadays, there are of course royal relations who seem to be more strenuously employed than is the Queen Mother herself. Nevertheless, the Senior Lady remains industrious in her own way, whether attending to her horses and her racing or to the country's arts and charities, to honorific ceremonial, and certainly to giving more than token encouragement to literally hundreds of very varied Good Causes.

She does not undertake many far travels now – though Canada, uniquely welcoming and possessive about her, has remained the exception. Ontario insisted that Montreal and the Black Watch should not have it all their own way, and irresistibly invited her to visit the capital province next.

And who else but the Queen Consort of wartime could better be appointed to go over to Normandy forty-five years after that June 6 of 1944 which began the great liberation of German-dominated Europe? Her Majesty unveiled a D-Day Memorial window in Bayeux Cathedral on the exact anniversary, noting that Bayeux was the first town in the north of that Continent across the English Channel to be liberated by the Allies. And later there was a linked home engagement: the Normandy Veterans Association, through its East Kent branch, invited her to unveil a commemorative window in Canterbury Cathedral.

Memorable occasions within the United Kingdom included

For years, each August the Fourth has brought original home-made birthday cards, as well as flowers, to Her Majesty as she comes out from the Clarence House gates and people who have waited for hours rush towards her with their gifts.

the marking of her first ten years as Lord Warden and Admiral of the Cinque Ports and Constable of Dover Castle. This meant a ceremonial visit to Dover (sailing into the harbour aboard H.M. Yacht *Britannia*) to be present at a weighty gathering of the dignitaries of those ancient towns on the Kent and Sussex coasts. The main event, after a thanksgiving service in church, a full meeting of the Ports' delightfully named 'Court of Brotherhood and Guestling' at which the Confederation presented a loyal address to the royal Lord Warden.

As to domestic life in the Royal Family, a renewal of the importance of Sandringham as a royal residence must have given quiet pleasure to Queen Elizabeth. She has always had affectionate attachment to the rambling great house in windswept Norfolk: it was her husband's birthplace and he, King George VI, used to say that it was the home where he was always happy. And at Sandringham it was that he drew his last breath.

During the present reign the house had a long run of Christmas gatherings there; but in the Seventies, with the family's numbers increasing fast (and the remoteness and overnighting inconveniences of Sandringham being remarked on!), Windsor Castle, easy of access and with plenty of suitable rooms, became each year the scene of the December celebrations. Then, recently, there came a Christmas switch back to Sandringham and the various buildings in the grounds of the estate.

The reason? It had become very necessary that a gradual and years-long re-wiring and refurbishing of Windsor Castle be undertaken: which meant many rooms out of action, uninhabitable because of workmen's operations, and not

available to the many branches of 'the Royals' and their domestic staffs. In short, old Windsor – in boarding-house terms – couldn't 'sleep as many as usual'. (Incidentally, other upheavals lately at the Castle have involved the famous Round Tower, built on the mound where William the Conqueror established his fort above the River Thames nine hundred years ago. It had been discovered that the old foundations of the Tower were sinking into the ground, and that there was real danger, as it gradually tilted, that the whole of the massive stone structure, already cracking, would more and more become the *Leaning* Tower of Windsor. In short, it was liable to a disastrous break, and nothing but a major subterranean reinforcing of the building would save it. The offices inside the Tower had to be evacuated and its workers – keepers, registrars and curators of The Queen's Archives – forced to remove themselves and their records elsewhere.)

So, yet another generation of young 'Royals' – Prince William and Prince Harry and their young contemporaries – have come to experience East Anglian life at Sandringham, very different from Windsor and London, and to enjoy from time to time the rural pleasures of the Norfolk house which was bought and built upon by that ancestor of theirs, the popular 'Teddy', the Prince of Wales who became King Edward VII.

Meanwhile, at the moment of writing, neither Clarence

House, St. James's, nor Royal Lodge in Berkshire is sustaining armies of workmen or subsiding into the subsoil: the Queen Mother's residences stand firm.

Which is a contented note on which to draw towards the end of this book. And it is tempting to me, finally, to instance the value of our Mother Queen by quirky reference to assessments of her from other minds than mine.

Lasting Lustre

The lady's stock stays high, untainted in a soiled and insecure world, part of which – if stirred-up controversies in some newspapers are to be noticed – has a feeling that certain members of 'the Royals' are expensive and expendable free-wheelers. But republicanism continues to be a dead duck in Britain; and in the frequent opinion polls on popular personalities which are familiar Press gimmicks the First Family usually fill most of the top ten places, with the Queen Mother always high in that grade.

It is an interesting point. Investigative journalists discover that in these days royalty in general means almost nothing at all to some of the new generation. Nothing, for instance, to many of the thousands of disco-deafened inner city youngsters; and yet, when the quizzing brings up references to 'the Queen Mum',

Above The Black Watch are 'her own', her Scots family's Highland regiment, and Her Majesty has been Colonel-in-Chief ever since she was crowned Queen Consort. Thus the year 1987 brought the fiftieth anniversary of that honour; and Queen Elizabeth went to Berlin, where the first battalion was stationed, to mark the occasion.

Opposite In 1988 the Royal Family's Christmas gathering was not at Windsor as usual, but at Sandringham. So attendance at Christmas morning service was at the parish church there in rural Norfolk. Here are four generations of the House of Windsor emerging from the church door.

mumbles of actual approval of the monarchy emerge, even if only in opinions that the institution is an 'okay tourist attraction' and anyway 'one of the things we've got that's not made in Japan or Taiwan'!

A more relevant personal note might be added. The fact that the Queen Mother has lasting lustre was newly borne upon the present writer when the driver of a London taxicab, on being paid off at a Clarence House door, wagged a head knowingly and said: 'Lucky you, sir, going to see her. She's a great old stick.' The intended if inelegant tribute was overheard and was

eported to the Old Stick herself, who went into peals of aughter.

She does not spend time in counting her richness in years; and, ndeed, when inside her door and in the orbit of that smile of velcome, notions of elderliness become ridiculous. Magazine rticles proclaiming 'Britain's oldest-ever Queen – Now well xceeding Victoria' do not seem to be about anybody present.

Yes, Victoria was old – deliberately, professionally old, and for a very long time. Queen Elizabeth the Queen Mother is not like that at all, simply because she is quite uninterested in the age business. It is as simple as that.

Let others weary over the arithmetic. For her, there is a 'new every morning' embrace of each returning day. Another twenty-four hours to live for, work for, and enjoy.

The Queen Mother even managed a visit to troubled Northern Ireland in '88 to open the National Trust property at Castle Coole in County Fermanagh. For the cutting of a ceremonial ribbon, the Visitor was presented with a pair of scissors by the two-year-old son of the Earl and Countess, Lord and Lady Belmore.

The smile, the gesture – it could be no-one else.

Index

Page numbers in *italics* indicate captions to illustrations

Photographic acknowledgments

Reproduced by gracious permission of Her Majesty The Queen 24, 41, 44 top, 48 bottom, 71 bottom, 75 top, 78 bottom, 79 top and bottom; Associated Newspapers, London 134 top, 156; Associated Press, London 163; BIPNA, London 149, 150 top; Camera Press, London 34, 60, 88, 127 top, 136 bottom, 177: Peter Abbey 158, Prince Andrew 182 top and bottom, Cecil Beaton 47, Jim Bennett 125 bottom, 131 bottom, 166, Alan Davidson 144, 165, Michel Guntern 131 top, Glenn Harvey 178 bottom, Patrick Lichfield 154–5, Bernard Morton 186, Richard Open 13 bottom, Norman Parkinson 128 top, 140, Geoffrey Shakerley 12, Richard Slade 127 bottom, Lord Snowdon 8, Albert Watson 179, Alex Wilson 170 right; Lord Adam Gordon 98 top left; Tim Graham, London 136 top, 142, 150 bottom; Major John Griffin 101; Captain R. Grimshaw 94–5; Hulton Deutsch Collection, London 16, 33, 40 top, 42 bottom, 45, 46, 50 bottom, 56, 59, 64, 65, 66 top and bottom, 67 bottom, 72 top, 74 top, 76 top, 77, 78 top, 83 top and bottom, 84–5, 87 top and bottom, 90 bottom, 91, 92, 96, 97, 100, 103 bottom right, 104, 108 top, 110 top, 111, 112 bottom, 128 bottom, 130 top, 133 bottom, 134 bottom, 135 top, 137, 152, 153, 174, 180 top, 183 top; Imperial War Museum, London 74 bottom; A. F. Kersting, London 22 bottom; The Octopus Group 28, 29, 31 top, 38, 40 bottom, 48 top, 52, 58, 70, 71 top, 73 top and bottom, 76 bottom: Michael Plomer 2, 10, 11, 14–15, 19, 20 top and bottom, 22 top, 23, 26 bottom, 27, 30, 54, 55, 79 top and bottom, 98 top right and bottom, 114 top and bottom, 115 top and bottom, 118 top and bottom, 119, 120, 143, 146, 189; Pacemaker Press International, Belfast 188; Popperfoto, London 36 top and bottom, 43, 49, 51 top and bottom, 53, 61, 62 top, 63, 67 top, 68, 80, 89, 90 top, 103 bottom left, 106 bottom left, 109; Press Association, London 32, 125 top, 132, 148, 162; Rex Features, London 151; Save the Children Fund, London 126 bottom: Mark Bowden 129; John Scott 86, 99, 102 top, 106 top, 110 bottom, 122, 138, 139, 147, 171; Syndication International, London 13 top, 62 bottom, 105, 107 top and bottom, 108 bottom, 112 top, 113, 117, 124, 126 top, 130 bottom, 133 top, 135 bottom, 141, 157, 159 top and bottom, 160, 161 top and bottom, 164, 167, 168–9, 169, 170 left, 172, 175 top and bottom, 176, 178 top, 180 bottom, 181, 183 bottom, 185, 187; The Times, London 82; Windsor Archives 24, 41, 42 top, 44 top and bottom, 48 bottom, 71 bottom, 72 bottom, 75 top.